AF559907

SCHOOL CURRICULUM AND ADMINISTRATION

Books by the same authors published by Discovery Publishing House

School Curriculum

Elementary Curriculum

Language Arts Curriculum

Philosophy and Curriculum

Psychology and Curriculum

Improving School Administration

School Curriculum and Administration

Teaching English Successfully

Teaching Mathematics Successfully

Teaching Science Successfully

Teaching Social Studies Successfully

Teaching Language Arts Successfully

Teaching Mathematics in Elementary Schools

Teaching Science in Elementary Schools

Teaching Social Studies in Elementary Schools

ENCYCLOPAEDIA OF SCHOOL CURRICULUM - VIII

SCHOOL CURRICULUM AND ADMINISTRATION

By

Dr. Marlow Ediger
M.S. Education, Ph.D.
Professor Emeritus in Education
Truman State University
Box 417, 201 W, 22nd St
North Newton KS 67117
United States of America

&

Dr. Digumarti Bhaskara Rao
M.Sc., M.A., M.A., M.Ed., Ph.D.
Reader & Research Director
R.V.R. College of Education
Srinivasa Nagar Colony
Guntur–522 006
(India)

DISCOVERY PUBLISHING HOUSE PVT. LTD.
NEW DELHI-110 002

First Published – 2003

Reprinted – 2018

ISBN: 978-93-5056-597-1 (Set)

ISBN: 978-81-7141-709-4

Published by:

DISCOVERY PUBLISHING HOUSE PVT. LTD.

4383/4B, Ansari Road Darya Ganj
New Delhi - 110 002 (India)
Phone: +91-11-23279245, 43596064-65
Fax: +91-11-23253475
E-mail: discoverypublishinghouse@gmail.com
sales@discoverypublishinggroup.com
web: www.discoverypublishinggroup.com

Printed at:
Infinity Imaging Systems
Delhi

Dedicated
to
People's Doctor

Dr. Kondabolu Basava Punnaiah
M.B., B.S.

Preface

The school curriculum and administration are closely interwoven and each of one's success depends on each one's effective implementation. The totality curricular experiences are to be provided to students through efficient school administration. Then only will the schools flourish by nourishing their student clientele effectively.

This book on school curriculum and administration is written to introduce some useful innovative ideas into the minds of the curriculum designers and educational administrators, which help in providing effective schooling to students.

The ideas expressed in this book will be useful to curriculum designers, book writers, teachers, educational planners, school administrators and others in developing good schools.

Prof. Marlow Ediger

Dr. Digumarti Bhaskara Rao

Contents

	Preface	*V*
1.	Upgraded School Administrators	1
2.	Student Reentry into the Curriculum	7
3.	In-Service Education : In Which Direction?	15
4.	The Urban School Curriculum	23
5.	Improving the Rural School Curriculum	29
6.	School Administration and the Curriculum	35
7.	Student Motivation in Reading	44
8.	Priorities in the Social Studies	51
9.	Psychology in Teaching Mathematics	58
10.	The Integrated Science Curriculum	66
11.	The Administrator as an Instructional Leader	77
12.	Remedying Ills in Society	84
13.	Parent-Teacher Conferences and the Pupil	91
14.	Administrators and the School Secretary	95
15.	Philosophy of Kindergarten Education	101
16.	Issues in Microcomputer Use in the Classroom	109
17.	The Counsellor in the School Curriculum	120
18.	Problem Solving and the School Administrator	126
19.	Using the School Library	135
	Additional Reading	*144*
	Index	*155*

1

Upgraded School Administrators

School administration is a complex endeavor. Increased responsibilities are in the offing for school administrators. Changing trends in education as well as new laws for the public (government) schools require competence in the field of school administration.

Needed—Knowledgeable Administrators

Teachers tend to be better educated than ever before. Teachers with masters degrees and higher are common in the schools. It behooves the school administrator to be highly knowledgeable in the educational arena. Personal biases and prejudices are not adequate to be leaders of public schools.

Recently, a school administrator announced to teachers a new goal for students to achieve. Thus, all students within three years were to achieve on the ninetieth or higher percentile, according to the standardized achievement tests presently being administered. The administrator believed in high academic standards for students. Selected teachers being highly knowledgeable about statistics began to question the reality of the goal. The school administrator did not back down on his stated goal.

After the meeting, numerous teachers began to discuss how students in the school were to be on the ninetieth percentile or higher within three years, based on the presently administered standardized achievement tests. Questioned raised by teachers included the following :

1. Did the student population in the local school district represent a somewhat normal distribution?
2. If the local school population closely resembles a normal distribution, how is it possible to have students achieve on the ninetieth percentile or higher? Fifty per cent of the students normally would be above and fifty per cent below the fiftieth percentile.
3. Should it be possible for local students to attain on the ninetieth percentile or higher, did teachers teach specifically for the items on the test?
4. What kind of education are students receiving if teachers teach isolated bits of information, so that administrators may look good in terms of student achievement?
5. Are tests of such ultimate importance that measurable results only are important in reporting student progress to parents?

As a school example of needing more knowledgeable administrators, a teacher at a faculty meeting mentioned selected ways of organising the curriculum. These were the separate subjects, the correlated, the fused, and the integrated curriculum. The administrator chairing the faculty meeting was not aware of degrees of relating subject-matter in teaching. He accused the teacher of making up something to support her thinking to improve the curriculum. Other faculty members made no comments to support or refute the reality of organising the curriculum in terms of the separate subjects, correlated, fused, or integrated curricula.

Pertaining to knowledge in organising the curriculum, the writers recommend the following for training school administrators:

1. School administrators need to take adequate course work on university campuses pertaining to diverse facets of curriculum development, educational psychology, and philosophy of education.
2. School administrators prior to certification must pass rigid competency tests on curriculum development.
3. School administrators should experience a demanding internship pertaining to all facets of developing the curriculum.

Facets of Developing the Curriculum

As a third example of needing more knowledgeable administrators in schools, loyalty to the profession of education is lacking. For example, a state has developed and mandated the giving of tests to students in the public school on diverse grade levels. The state mandated test was not tried out in a pilot study. Thus, the concepts of item analysis, validity, and reliability are completely lacking. Formerly, a standardized test of renown was given yearly to students in selected grades within a specific school district. The school administrator announced to teachers in a faculty meeting that the state mandated test was very much superior in quality to the standardized test.

Selected teachers at the faculty meeting raised questions about the state mandated test having no data available to support its merits, whereas the standardized test has excellent data on standard deviation, percentile ranks, the norm group, how test items were selected, as well as validity and reliability statistics.

School administrators in these situations are either ill informed about tests and testing, or they are sacrificing professional knowledge for political gains. Political gains emphasize supporting a point of view, such as statewide testing, regardless of their quality. State-wide tests must meet the same criteria as compared to reputable standardized tests. Validity and reliability data need to be clearly spelled out for both state mandated and standardized tests, be they criterion referenced or norm referenced.

Needed-School Administrators with Social Skills

School administrators work with diverse personalities involving certified and non-certified personnel. If an administrator is able to work effectively with a few teachers only, this is not adequate.

School administrators in pre-service education need to experience working with teachers of diverse personal and social traits. In pre-service programmes these teachers should appraise administrator behaviour in terms of clearly stated objectives. Prospective administrators who do not work effectively with teachers and other workers in the school setting should not be licensed or certified. The school setting represents a social setting. There are teachers and other specialists, as well as custodians, cafeteria workers, aides, and students. Being able to work effectively with others is a definite necessity.

Deficiencies among administrators in working well with others in school include the following:

1. Favouring a few teachers with positive comments and praise.
2. Recognizing selected teachers at faculty meetings and ignoring comments of others.
3. Listening carefully to a few teachers on ideas in conducting a workshop. Other teachers, according to the principal, hardly know anything about procedures and topics to be covered in the workshop.
4. Holding in esteem the school secretary or secretaries above that of classroom teachers and other specialists in the educational arena.

Needed—Administrators with Positive Attitudes

School administrators need to possess positive attitudes towards people in school and in society. Positive attitudes toward educating students is a must. School administrators who stay put in their offices during the school day need to experience a change of attitudes. Each administrator needs to provide leadership, guidance, and assistance to teachers to provide the best curriculum possible for each learner. Human beings have much worth and need to have their talents and abilities developed fully. Creativity on the part of school workers is a must. The administrator needs to assist teachers and other certified as well as non-certified individuals, achieve as much as possible within the school setting.

Pertaining to developing positive attitudes within school administrators, the following seem pertinent:

1. Pre-service university programmes in school administration should strongly emphasize selecting and retaining principals and superintendents with quality feelings, beliefs, and values.
2. Principals and superintendents need to be appraised by teachers and other professionals on vital criteria pertaining to leadership qualities in the school setting.

3. School administrators should demonstrate qualities of having desirable attitudes, prior to employment.

Needed—Moral Standards and Professional Behaviour in Schools

Mandates by states in determining objectives and tests for students should be greatly minimized or eliminated. Well trained and educated teachers and administrators need to be heavily involved on the local level in selecting objectives, learning activities, and appraisal procedures for students. It makes no professional sense to have a state, removed from the local school, determine what students are to learn (objectives of instruction) as well as develop tests to measure student progress. Too frequently, the test results become absolute. No other appraisal procedures are appreciated or valued. Report cards may be issued by the state in comparing one district against another, based on state mandated test results. Even, within a school district, the achievement of one school against another is made. This is wrong. School districts differ much from each other in terms of wealth, opportunity, and levels of education of students. Within a school district, students in one building come from more favourable educational environments, as compared to students of another school building. Students then in one school district do not start at the same beginning point as do students in another district. Neither do students in one building start at the same beginning point as do students in another building. The race for achievement is then unfair, since students do not start at the same place. Talented and gifted students have an initial advantage over other students. They are ahead of others when the race is started in comparing one school district against another, or one building of students against another.

Recommendations to Improve Schools

Numerous recommendations are made to improve the school curriculum:

1. School teachers and administrators, being well educated and trained, should be heavily involved in selecting objectives, learning activities and appraisal.
2. Competition be in evidence to hire the best teachers possible. Good teachers could then be hired away from other school districts. Teachers of excellence should be adequately recruited for.

3. Good teachers should have a low enough teacher-student ratio so the former can teach well and the latter may achieve optimally. A good teacher cannot do well with an excess number of students in a classroom.

4. Teachers of excellence should have up-to-date textbooks and other reference sources to provide for individual difference in a classroom.

5. Classrooms, comfortable and conducive to teaching, is a must. Leaky roofs, and loud banging steam radiators do not assist pupils to attain well in ongoing lessons and units.

6. The burden should largely be on the school board and the lay public to be accountable. Too frequently, teachers have been held accountable for student progress regardless of the surrounding situations involved. Inadequate teaching materials, large class size, and low salaries hinder motivation on the part of teachers to do a good job of teaching.

7. Stated mandated tests should be minimized and even brought to a complete halt. The isolated facts and subject matter learned by students, as emphasized by state mandated tests, does not reflect what educational psychologist recommend in the curriculum. Students should be guided to perceive that knowledge is related and not isolated in terms of bits of information to be learned.

2

Student Reentry into the Curriculum

Much is written about students who drop out of school prior to or after receiving a high school diploma. The future for these students is rather dismal. The W.T. Grant Foundation financed a study of individuals entering the work place with a high school diploma or less in terms of formal schooling. Their report *The Forgotten Half: Non-College Bound Youth in America*[1] stresses the following bleak future of approximately 20 million young Americans who are not likely to attend college.

> In 1986 males between the ages of 20 and 24 who had high school diplomas and were employed earned 28 per cent less in constant dollars than a comparable group in 1973. The income decline was 24 per cent for white males and 44 per cent for black males.
>
> High school dropouts have suffered an even larger income decline. In 1986 dropouts between the ages of 20 and 24 earned 42 per cent less in constant dollars than a comparable group in 1973.
>
> In 1984, 12 per cent of all males between the ages of 20 and 24 said that they had no income, up from 7.3 per cent in 1973.
>
> In 1973, 60 per cent of all employed young males earned incomes high enough to support a three-person family above the poverty level, but by 1985 only 43.7 per cent earned incomes that high.

> The proportion of males under age 24 who were not in college and who were working full-time dropped from 73 per cent in 1974 to 49 per cent in 1986. Similarly, the proportion of young females who were not in college and who were working full time fell from 57 per cent in 1968 to 42 per cent in 1986.
>
> Of the 3.1 million households headed by youths under age 25 in 1985, 30 per cent had incomes below the poverty level—nearly double the percentage in the early 1970s. (Given this fact, it is not surprising that the marriage rate among all 20 to 24 year-olds fell 46 per cent between 1974 and 1985—and fell a full 62 per cent among blacks.)

The above data is indeed is disheartening. Students who have left the education arena need identification. These students need encouragement to come back to complete formal education programmes, necessary for personal success and achievement in life. A quality curriculum needs to be in the offing. The curriculum for the reentry students must emphasize relevant objectives. These ends need to be perceived as vital by students. Learning opportunities to attain the chosen objectives must meet criteria of being purposeful, meaningful, and of interest to the learner.

As effective means of appraisal needs to be in the offing to determine the progress of the reentry student. Diverse methods of appraisal should be emphasized. Intellectual, emotional, social and physical facets of learner progress need to be appraised thoroughly. Quality attitudes should be significant outcomes of the evaluation process. Counselling and guidance services offered by a qualified, sympathetic, and caring person must be available to the reentry student.

Placement services are a must after the reentry student has completed course requirements. These students should not be allowed to sink or swim. Rather, success and assistance should be key concepts in guiding the reentry student into the world of work, be it a vocation, occupation, profession, or additional levels of formal education.

Identification of Prospective Reentry Students

Students leaving any level of formal education need to be identified. Reasons for their leaving need to be determined. Reasons generally inherent as to why students leave formal education include the following:

1. earn money;
2. lack of interest;
3. failure to perceive purpose or reasons for attending;
4. lack of goal clarity;
5. pregnancy;
6. loneliness;
7. no friends;
8. low grades;
9. problems in the home setting;
10. marriage.

Counsellors need to discuss with the potential reentry student as to reasons for leaving formal education. Respecting the thinking of others is important. In an atmosphere of understanding, the counsellor and the individual need to evaluate the merits for reentering formal education programmes. If the student again enrolls in course work, the counsellor must periodically assess if needs of the former are being met. The sink or swim beliefs for reentry student must be minimized. These at risk students need assistance in securing adequate money to finance formal education, as well as perceive interest, purpose, and goal clarity in the curriculum. Problems of pregnancy, loneliness and lack of friends need to be discussed openly with the counsellor. Agreed upon solutions to each identified problem should be an end result.

Encouragement needs to be given if the reentry student has experienced a low grade point average when previously attending school. Talking with the student about home problems may assist the learner to realize that there is sympathy and empathy when discouragement sets in. Adequate paying part-time jobs may need arranging when finances are a problem and/or the reentered student is married or is contemplating marriage.

A tremendous investment of money and time is necessary to assist individuals to reenter the halls of learning. Working at dead end, low paying jobs hinder any person from achieving and progressing. Society loses out on talents and abilities in these situations. The individual as well as society should benefit when the reentry student is pursuing definite objectives in completing course requirements.

Curriculum for the Reentry Student

The reentry student needs assistance in pursuing course work leading to graduation. Positive reinforcement needs to be given to these students for achieving well. Diagnosis and remediation are necessary for reentry students who are not progressing at a satisfactory rate. Individual differences need to be provided for. Thus, slow, average, and fast learners individually must pursue course offerings which provide for success in learning. Challenge needs to be in the offing for each learner to attain as much as possible. Time on task and optimal achievement should be the lot of each student.

To have reentry students achieve well, they must experience:

1. *a curriculum which is of interest*. Dull, boring courses will hinder these students from staying on in the educational arena. Interesting materials and methods of teaching should be the lot of each reentry student;
2. *purpose in learning*. Reasons for achieving are accepted by the student. Not perceiving purpose for learning makes for low motivation in ongoing activities;
3. *meaningful course work*. If a student attaches meaning to ongoing instruction, he/she understands content being taught. Meaningless presentations make for feelings of failure among students;
4. *balance among objectives*. Thus, three categories of objectives are being emphasized in the curriculum. These are understandings, skills, and attitudes. With achieved understandings objectives students acquire facts, concepts and generalizations. To utilize the facts, concepts, and generalizations, skill objectives need to be stressed. Doing sometimes with the understandings acquired emphasizes skill development. To do the very best in life, quality attitudes must be developed by students. Good attitudes assist in achieving well in understandings and skills objectives.

Within a quality curriculum for the reentry student, philosophies of education which assist each to attain as much as possible should be emphasized. Four philosophies are relevant for teachers to implement, in whole or in part. Thus, the reentry student needs to experience problem solving. Problem solving skills are important to use in school and in society. Life in its diverse manifestations consists of identifying and solving problems. Flexible steps of problem solving include:

1. identifying the problem;
2. gathering data in answer to the problem;
3. developing a hypothesis;
4. testing the hypothesis;
5. revising the hypothesis, if needed.

Problem solving philosophies emphasize:

1. integrating the school curriculum and society;
2. stressing committee or group endeavour in solving problems, as is done in society;
3. harmonizing the interests of students with effort in learning. With interest in problem identification, effort is then put forth in learning by reentry students;
4. learners selecting realistic problem to solve. The teacher is a guide and stimulator;
5. realizing that solutions to problems have their own consequences.

A second philosophy stresses individual decision-making. A learning centre's methodology of instruction may here be in evidence. From an ample number of centres and tasks, the individual student selects which learning opportunities to pursue. Time on task is salient. The chooser omits tasks not harmonizing with personal interests, needs, and abilities. Students may select tasks emphasizing problem solving or knowledge for its own sake. Generally, tasks selected stress the making of individual moral choices. Decisions are subjective and not objective choices. How the individual chooses does affect others.

Decision-making philosophies stress:

1. an endless number of options open to the chooser;
2. each person developing his/her own purposes in life. The purposes are not given to any individual;
3. student-teacher planning of the curriculum;
4. life itself presents absurd situations. Within the subjective and the absurd, decisions need to be made;
5. the importance of personal choices affecting others.

A third philosophy emphasizes the testing and measurement movement school of thought. With the testing and measurement movement, pre-determined precise objectives for preentry students need to be in the offing. The precise ends must emphasize new content or skills to be achieved. And yet, the objectives should be achievable. A pretest can adjust the reentry student's curriculum to where he/she is presently. Pretest results for each student indicate present instructional levels. These students may then achieve sequential objectives at a rate conducive to optimal achievement levels. The instructor selects the learning opportunities to have reentry students attain the precise ends. Evaluation of each student's achievement is done in terms of stated objectives. Remedial work is given if a student does not attain a specific objective.

Testing and measurement movements emphasize:

1. pre-determined specific objectives for students to attain;
2. evaluation of what is observable and varifiable. What is internal to the student cannot be evaluated;
3. criterion and norm referenced tests be utilized to ascertain student achievement. Criterion referenced tests (CRT's) will be utilized most frequently since they harmonize with a specific set of behaviourally stated objectives developed prior to instruction;
4. objectivity in the appraisal processes. Subjective means of appraisal are frowned upon;
5. students meeting definite standards of achievement.

A fourth philosophy of teaching for reentry students stresses a subject centred curriculum. Having students learn content, concepts, and generalizations are paramount in teaching. The abstract is preferable to the concrete and the semi-concrete.

In learning vitable subject matter, mental development of reentry students has become the major objective of teaching and learning. Cultivation of the intellect of students is inherent in ongoing lessons and units. Cognitive objectives, rather than affective or psychomotor learnings are emphasized in the curriculum. Affective and psychomotor goals are significant only to the point and place where cognitive development of reentry students is fostered. The mind needs stimulation, challenge, and encouragement to guide reentry students to acquire much subject matter.

A subject centred approach in teaching reentry students stresses:

1. an idea centred curriculum. Vital concepts and generalizations need to be attained by reentry students;
2. cultivation of the intellect and mental development of learners as major goals of instruction;
3. challenge, motivation, and encouragement to attain well academically;
4. well qualified teachers, academically inclined, be involved in curriculum development and implementation;
5. utilization of carefully selected basal textbooks, single or multiple series, together with other reference materials to assist students in goal attainment.

In evaluating each philosophy of education in teaching reentry students, the following appear salient:

1. problem solving skills are important in the school curriculum, as well as in the societal arena;
2. decision making on an individual basis and developing one's own purposes in life are salient. Life consists of making choices where subjectivity prevails. Moral decisions emphasize the subjective facets of life, personally as well as in interacting with others;
3. precise objectives need attainment if they are vital, relevant, and do not emphasize isolated bits of content to be learned. Adequate stress also needs to be placed on the attitudinal or affective development of reentry students;

4. cultivation of the intellect as a sole objective may not meet the personal needs of the reentry student. Subject matter must be useful and utilitarian for students who have left and come back to complete course requirements.

In Closing

The reentry student, as is true of all human beings, has tremendous worth. These students ultimately need to earn an adequate income to sustain the self and members in the family. Income earned should make for an enriched life of self-fulfilment. Work performed in society, after graduation, should be satisfying and rewarding. The self in society needs to experience success and happiness.

Note

1. As quoted in *Phi Delta Kappan*. Bloomington, Indiana: Phi Delta Kappa, February, 1988, Pages 404-414. The total report has 104 pages.

REFERENCES

Cruickshank, Donald R. *Teaching is Tough*. Englewood Cliffs, New Jersey: Prentice-Hall, Inc., 1980.

Henson, Kenneth T. *Secondary Teaching Methods*. Lexington, Massachusetts: D.C. Heath and Company, 1981.

Joyce, Bruce, and Marsha Weil. *Models of Teaching*. Third Edition. Englewood Cliffs, New Jersey: Prentice-Hall, Inc., 1986.

Joyce, Bruce, *et al*. *The Structure of School Improvement*. New York: Longmans, 1983.

National Society for the Study of Education. *Staff Development*, Part II. Chicago, Illinois: The Society, 1983.

National Society for the Study of Education. *The Humanities in Precollegiate Education*, Part II. Chicago, Illinois: The Society, 1984.

National Society for the Study of Education. *Education in School and Non-School Setting*, Part I. Chicago, Illinois: The Society, 1985.

National Society for the Study of Education. *The Ecology of School Renewal*, Part I. Chicago, Illinois: The Society, 1987.

National Society for the Study of Education. *Society as Education in an Age of Transition*, Part II. Chicago, Illinois: The Society, 1987.

Phi Delta Kappan. *The Forgotten Half: Non-College Bound Youth in America*. Bloomington, Indiana: Phi Delta Kappa, February, 1988, pp. 404-414.

3

In-Service Education: In Which Direction?

Frequent mention is made for the necessity of in-service education for teachers. Thus, workshops, faculty meetings, and peer coaching, among other approaches to in-service education, are elaborated up in professional educational journals, as well as in the news media. "There needs to be change in education", is a constant slogan. The lay public "does not want to pay for more of the same kind of teaching; they want reform".

A major problem arises pertaining to what is meant by reform in education. It is quite apparent that there are reforms (plural) and not reform (singular). Truth in terms of reform is education, resides within the beholder. Uniform concepts of reform do not exist. The balance of this paper will examine diverse philosophies as to what constitutes reform.

The Testing and Measurement Movement

Advocates of reform in education may stress the importance of students achieving at a higher level on tests. A student then is doing well if his/her test scores on criterion and/or norm referenced tests are going up. Workshops and faculty meetings are held in a school on ways that teachers can assist students to do better on tests. Students may then take one or more classes on how to take tests. One school may be compared against another school within a system as to which has higher student test scores. The state may issue a report card as to comparisons made on how well students in one school system achieve on administered tests as compared to others. New superintendents and principals have been hired to up student test scores within a school district. Test scores have risen dramatically in these situations.

The testing and measurement movement emphasizes:

1. observable results from students in terms of higher scores on tests. What happens within the student, such as interests, feelings, and attitudes, is of little importance;
2. competition among students, schools, and school systems within a state. The feeling tends to be that competition alone brings out the best from the students;
3. predetermined objectives for student attainment. These objectives may be developed on the state level, the district level such as instructional management system (IMS), or by the teacher prior to instruction. The testing and measurement movement leaves little, if any, leeway' for learner input into the curriculum;
4. measurement of student progress against the predetermined objectives. Emergent objectives or student-teacher planning has little or no value in the testing and measurement movement;
5. students achieving lower level cognitive objectives. Attitudes do not receive much emphasis. One reason for the lack of emphasis is the inherent difficulties in writing specific, measurable attitudinal objectives. Higher level cognitive objectives, such as critical and creative thinking, as well as problem solving create difficult situations when writing these kinds of ends in behavioural terms with indicators revealing minimal levels of attainment.

Testing and measurement philosophy merely represents one school of thought in terms of objectives, learning opportunities, and evaluation procedures in the curriculum. Other philosophies also need to be considered.

Problem Solving in the Curriculum

Problem solving is a process. Something happens within the individual as he/she engages in problem solving activities. The processes involved in problem solving are not measurable and cannot be tested. Several models can be given for flexible steps of problem solving. One model stresses the following criteria:

1. identifying and clarifying a problem;
2. gathering data or information from a variety of reference sources in attempts to solve the problem;
3. developing a hypothesis which reflects answers to the problem;
4. testing the hypothesis in a life-like situation;
5. revising the hypothesis, if necessary.

New problems can arise within the framework of any of the above-named steps. Answers to problems are tentative and not absolutes. Thought and action are integrated, not separate entities. Thus, when problems are clarified and related data gathered, something is done with the results. That something involves testing the hypothesis in a life-like situation and receiving needed feedback to make possible modifications in future courses of action.

One can only experience, but not know the real world as it truly exists and is in problem solving philosophies. Problem solving stress that students identify and solve real, life-like problems, as they exist in society. The school curriculum and society are one and not separate domains. The problems may also be stimulated to provide for a miniature society in school.

In-service education stressing problem solving is quite different from testing and measurement movements. The teacher emphasizing problem solving realizes that predetermined objectives for students to achieve do not advocate students identifying and attempting to solve realistic problems in society.

An Idea Centred Curriculum

An idea centred curriculum tends to emphasize mental development of students. The intellectual facet of a person's development is of utmost importance. Mind is real and needs to achieve optimally. Students then need to acquire vital subject matter. Reputable textbooks and other teaching materials used in the curriculum need to assist students to achieve worthwhile concepts and generalizations. Teaching materials need to focus on abstract content for learners to attain. The concrete and semi-concrete facets of learning are significant only to the degree that salient subject matter is acquired by students.

The teacher in an idea centred curriculum needs to be well trained and educated in the academic discipline taught. Teachers here need to select relevant subject matter objectives for students to achieve. Learning activities to achieve the chosen ends reflect the abstract so that students attain vital concepts and generalizations. Evaluation procedures need to ascertain how much students have learned and achieved in relationship to the stated objectives.

An idea centred curriculum emphasizes that:

1. persons cannot know the natural and social environment as it truly is. Rather, one receives ideas of the real world only. Thus, a subject centred curriculum with its emphasis upon ideas needs to be stressed in teaching-learning situations;
2. generalizations and concepts must receive major emphasis in students learning subject matter;
3. cultivation of the intellect should receive primary stress in the curriculum. Cognitive goals, rather than affective or psychomotor, should be predominant in teaching-learning situations;
4. textbooks, workbooks, and other abstract materials used as learning activities are more important as compared to the semi-concrete and concrete experiences;
5. in-service education for teachers should stress students achieving well in the cognitive or intellectual domain.

Looking to the Past for Direction

A look at what was relevant in the past and has survived in time and space may provide central themes for workshops and faculty meetings. The Great Books of the western world for secondary students and the Junior Great Books for elementary school pupils can provide objectives for student attainment. The works of these writers therein have stood the test of time (history) and place (geography).

Students need to have a challenging curriculum which emphasizes the great ideas of the past. The salient subject matter having stood the test of time and place becomes relevant for students. Content written in the present may not be important in the next few years. Much of what is written does not survive in significance. In a few years, the content is forgotten, never to be revived. Classical subject matter, however, remains important, regardless of place or time it was written. It takes durations of time to know if ideas written will survive. Thus, it is necessary to look to the past in terms of subject matter that great minds have thought. These salient ideas are as important now as they were in the past.

The Great Books advocate belief that:

1. What is vital to learn is the same, yesterday, today, and in the future. These timeless ideas students need to achieve.
2. Similar questions are raised by people, regardless of time and place. Classical content provides the necessary tools to understand society regardless of when or where the ideas were written.
3. Subject matter written needs to be appraised by members in society as to its worth. It might take centuries to ascertain worthwhile content for student attainment. Thus, for example, *The Republic* by Plato (427-347 B.C.), *Ethics and Politics* by Aristotle (384-322) and *The New Atlantis* by Francis Bacon (1561-1626) are examples of the classics which have survived in time and place.
4. Vital content needs to be learned by students. The enduring ideas are salient for students to acquire. The transitory and the insignificant need to be eliminated from the curriculum.
5. Workshops and faculty meetings need to encourage teacher interest and motivation in the classics. Classical subject matter must receive heavy emphasis in teaching-learning situations.

Decision-Making Skills for Students

Life in society demands that individuals become proficient in making decisions. Choices, from among alternatives, are made. To become proficient in decision-making, opportunities to practice this art must be in evidence throughout the school day.

Student-teacher planning of objectives, learning opportunities, and appraisal procedures may well emphasize decision-making by learners. Individualized reading is a second procedure in emphasizing decision-making. Here the student selects sequential trade books to read. He/she also plans the method of appraising progress, after having read a trade book from the reading centre. A third procedure in emphasizing student decision-making involves the utilization of learning centres. An adequate number of tasks must be available to students to emphasize time on task, as well as omitting those activities not deemed worthwhile. A third approach to stress in guiding student decision-making involves a contract system. The student with teacher guidance plans which learning opportunities should go into the contract. A due date for fulfilling the obligation in the contract is also established.

Decision-making philosophies stress the importance of:

1. students making choices in the curriculum. Students need to develop feelings of commitment in choosing and making selections;
2. subjectivity being involved in developing choices. From among alternatives, the learner needs to make moral decisions;
3. learners developing their own essences or purposes in life. Goals are not given to the student, but must be sought and found;
4. life itself not being rational in and of itself. Rather, the absurd may be experienced. Certainty cannot be attained in the curriculum and in life;
5. input coming from students in the total life of the school and in society.

In-service education approaches here must emphasize teachers and students being involved in selecting objectives, learning opportunities, and appraisal procedures.

In Closing

Selected philosophies or purposes in in-service education were discussed. These included:

1. testing and measurement movements;
2. problem solving procedures;
3. idea centred approaches;
4. classical emphasis;
5. decision-making practices.

Each of the above is different from the others as to scope and sequence in in-service education goals and objectives. Frequently, advocates of in-service education talk and write about the need for change in education. Little is said of the direction of change. If change in a specific direction is mentioned, it advocates higher test scores for students being an ultimate end. Certainly, problem solving and decision-making skills are just as salient. Problem solving and decision-making are necessary presently as well as in the future in school and in society. Subject matter in an idea centred curriculum or a classical curriculum is significant, particularly as they provide content in problem solving and decision-making. The testing and measurement movement is recommended if content on tests can be utilized in school and in society. In-service education programmes for teachers need to emphasize what is salient for students in the educational and societal arenas.

REFERENCES

Cruickshank, Donald R. *Teaching is Tough*. Englewood Cliffs, New Jersey: Prentice-Hall, Inc., 1980.

Henson, Kenneth T. *Secondary Teaching Methods*. Lexington, Massachusetts: D.C. Heath and Company, 1981.

Joyce, Bruce, and Marsha Weil. *Models of Teaching*. Third edition. Englewood Cliffs, New Jersey: Prentice-Hall, Inc., 1986.

Joyce, Bruce, *et al*. *The Structure of School Improvement*. New York: Longmans, 1983.

National Society for the Study of Education. *Staff Development*, Part II. Chicago, Illinois: The Society, 1983.

National Society for the Study of Education. *The Humanities in Precollegiate Education*, Part II. Chicago, Illinois: The Society, 1984.

National Society for the Study of Education. *Becoming Readers in a Complex Society*, Part I. Chicago, Illinois: The Society, 1984.

National Society for the Study of Education. *Education in School and Non-School Settings*, Part I. Chicago, Illinois: The Society, 1985.

National Society for the Study of Education. *The Ecology of School Renewal*, Part I. Chicago, Illinois: The Society, 1987.

National Society for the Study of Education. *Society as Education in an Age of Transition*, Part II. Chicago, Illinois: The Society, 1987.

4

The Urban School Curriculum

Students in urban schools need to achieve in an optimal manner. Teachers and administrators need to develop a psychology of learning which assists each student to learn as much as possible. There are selected principles of learning when followed by teachers should guide urban students to attain as much as possible.

Principles of Learning and the Urban School

First of all, teachers should assist students to develop and/or maintain interest in ongoing lessons and units. All other things being equal, students learn more when interested, as compared to a lack of interest. Each teacher needs to develop strategies of teaching which capture learner interest in the curriculum. Urban school students differ from each other in terms of which activities generate interest.

To secure student interest, it behooves the urban school teacher to utilize a variety of kinds of learning opportunities. Reading materials (textbooks, library books, and encyclopedias, among other printed media), as well as audio-visual aids (laser video disks, video tapes, slides, filmstrips, and films) should be used as learning activities so that urban students attain objectives. The media selected as a learning opportunity must capture the interests of the urban school student.

Secondly, learners in urban schools need to attach meaning to ongoing learning experiences. If these students understand what has been taught, meaning in ongoing lessons and units is in evidence. That which has meaning to a student relates directly to his/her past experiences. Content taught should come within the experiences of urban students so that relationships of new subject matter acquired with that previously taught is in evidence. Meaningful experiences, not rote learning of new subject matter, must be in the offing for the urban student.

Thirdly, the urban school student needs to experience success in learning. New subject matter needs to be learned by each student. And yet, the subject matter is attainable. If the content in ongoing lessons and units is too easy, boredom and a lack of challenge may be in evidence. Toward the other end of the continuum, if the content to be learned is excessively complex, failure to achieve may well be an end result.

Fourthly, purpose in learning is highly important. If an urban learner perceives purpose, reasons for learning and achieving are in evidence. Purpose may be acquired by students in a deductive manner. The teacher explaining briefly to students the value(s) inherent in learning new subject matter makes content more palitable for acquisition. In addition to deductive means of assisting students to perceive purpose in learning, inductive procedures may also be utilized. Through induction, the teacher raises questions of learners to assist the latter through discovery to perceive the importance of attaining vital facts, concepts, and generalizations.

Fifthly, urban students need to experience balance among objectives. Thus, cognitive, affective, and psychomotor objectives need to be emphasized in ongoing lessons and units. One category of objectives is not adequate of the three. Cognitive objectives (creative and critical thinking, problem solving, as well as acquiring vital facts, concept, and generalizations) are salient for learner achievement. School and society emphasize the importance of thinking skills to achieve optimally as fully functioning individuals. Affective ends advocate the importance of students having positive attitudes toward the self and toward others. Only then can cognitive objectives be achieved by students in an effective manner. Good attitudes also assist students to do well in the psychomotor dimension. Psychomotor growth emphasizes refined use of the gross and fine muscles, as well as attaining more optimally in manual dexterity. Urban students need to achieve well in cognitive, affective, and psychomotor domain objectives.

Utilizing principles of learning from research results in educational psychology should guide the teacher to help each student to achieve as much as possible.

The Philosophy of Education

Diverse philosophical schools of thought can do much to provide direction to urban teachers in selecting objectives, learning opportunities, and appraisal procedures.

Experimentalism, as one philosophy, emphasizes teachers guiding students in problem solving experiences. These problems should be life-like and real. What exists in society can provide excellent experiences in problem solving for students. With interest in problems selected, students should put forth effort in learning. Effort and interest become one and not separate entities.

Flexible, not absolute, steps of problem solving can be emphasized in ongoing lessons and units. These steps may include:

1. selecting a problem from among alternatives;
2. gathering data from diverse reference sources to secure tentative solutions or answers;
3. developing a hypothesis directly covering the gathered data or information;
4. testing the hypothesis in a realistic, not artificial, situation;
5. revising the hypothesis, if evidence warrants.

Urban school students need to experience problem solving in the curriculum. Learners will realize that in school and in society, problems are identified and attempted solutions made.

Idealism, as a second philosophy for the urban teacher to emphasize, advocates students achieving well in an idea centred curriculum. Intellectual development becomes salient in idealism. The mind is real and mental achievement of students needs to predominate in school.

The learning of subject matter is significant in idealism. Vital concepts and generalizations need to be selected by the teacher for student achievement. Textbooks, workshops, and other abstract reference materials should provide content for student acquisition. The teacher needs to be a true academic for students to be aided to achieve well. He/she serves as a model to help learners achieve well academically and intellectually. Abstract learning activities for students are prized more so than the concrete and the semi-concrete. However, concrete and semi-concrete activities should be brought into the curriculum as they guide students to learn more significant subject matter.

Urban school students need to achieve salient subject matter content and develop optimally in intellectual achievement.

Realism, as a third philosophy, emphasizes that one can know the real world as it truly is or exists. One then does not merely experience the real world as experimentalists emphasize, nor does the person only receive ideas pertaining to the actual natural and social world as idealistic believe. Rather, the carefully selected behaviourally stated objectives chosen by the urban teacher, among other individuals, and implemented in teaching-learning situations assist students to attain what is precise and measurable. The total number of objectives attained by students represents the scope of the curriculum. Sequence represents the order in which learners attain the objectives in the curriculum. Urban students need guidance to achieve as many specific objectives as individual abilities permit.

Existentialism, as a fourth philosophy, stresses students learning to choose and select on an individual basis. Decision-making becomes the number one goal. Life demands that to be human, each person must choose from among alternatives. If others make decisions for the self, one no longer is human, according to existentialism. The authentic self then makes decisions. Existentialists believe that life is ridiculous and absurd. However, within this environment, the human being chooses and selects from among alternatives options.

Urban students must have ample opportunities to make authentic selections. Among other methods of teaching, the following represent existentialist thinking:

1. a learning centre approach. Here, students may sequentially select tasks to complete. There are adequate tasks so that each student may omit those not deemed

beneficial. Time on task is highly important. An adequate number of tasks should deal with the human dilemma and condition. Values clarification then becomes important;

2. teacher-student planning of objectives, learning activities, and appraisal procedures. Heavy student input into curriculum development is important from an existentialist point of view;

3. contract systems. Each student plans learning opportunities with the teacher. These learning opportunities are placed on the contract. The student is heavily involved in terms of determining what he/she wishes to learn. The due date is written on the contract with attached student and teacher signature.

The learning centres approach, student-teacher planning of the curriculum, and the contract system emphasize a psychological, not logical, organisation of learning activities. Sequence resides within the student. Students order or sequence their very own experiences, resulting in a psychological curriculum.

Urban students need to be actively involved in ongoing lessons and units. Decision-making from among alternatives is the heart of the human condition.

In Closing

Urban students need to experience:

1. interesting activities in the curriculum;
2. meaning in ongoing lessons and units;
3. success in attaining objectives in the school setting;
4. purpose or reasons for learning;
5. cognitive, affective, and psychomotor goals in teaching-learning situations. Attaining one category of goals is not adequate. Balance among objectives needs to be stressed.

Pertaining to the philosophy of education, students in urban schools need to:

1. become proficient problem solvers in school and in society;
2. achieve dynamic, vital subject matter learnings in an idea centred curriculum;
3. attain relevant, not trivial, specific objectives in ongoing lessons and units;
4. develop proficiency in the decision-making area.

5

Improving the Rural School Curriculum

Rural areas can be hit hard with farm sales, farm foreclosures, and insolvencies. Prices for farm land and farm produce can go up and down rather rapidly. Two per cent of the total population live on farms and earn their living in whole or in part from farming. Larger farm machines to prepare the soil for seeding, harvest the farm crops, and feed livestock have made for situations where fewer farmers are needed, and, no doubt, even fewer will be needed in the years to come.

With negative income situations on many farms, young people in public schools will need to find future positions in the professions, vocations, and occupations. These positions will tend to take students from rural ways of living to where employment is available within urban centres. Students in rural schools need the very best education possible in order to be successful in the future in the world of work.

The Student and the Rural School Curriculum

Teachers of students in rural areas must follow definite principles of learning, from the psychology of education when ongoing lessons and units are in evidence.

A first principle of learning emphasizes that student interest is secured and maintained. A variety of learning opportunities are available to use in obtaining learner interest. Materials to utilize as learning opportunities include basal textbooks and library books as well as other printed materials; laser video discs and video tapes, films, filmstrips, slides, and single concept film loops; models, objects, excursions and realia in general; discussions, reports, panels, and other oral communication experiences; outlines, summaries, and written reports; as well as cassettes, tapes, and records.

A variety of learning opportunities is not utilized for the sake of doing so. But rather, the concept of *variety* is there to obtain the attention of students in teaching learning situations. Once students attend, the teacher needs to maintain learner interest in ongoing lessons and units. The rural school student needs to develop and maintain interest in the curriculum.

Secondly, the teacher needs to assist students to attach meaning to ongoing experiences. Learners must then understand what has been taught. If meaning is not attached to what has been learned, students fail to achieve and progress. Sequence in learning stresses that previously acquired knowledge provides readiness for new facts, concepts, or generalizations to be attained. A lack of understanding of subject matter presented will hinder a student from attaining sequential content in ongoing lessons and units. Students in rural schools then need to attach meaning and understanding to subject matter presented so that sequence in learning is in evidence.

Thirdly, students must perceive purpose in learning. To perceive purpose, learners accept reasons for achieving relevant facts, concepts, and generalizations. Energy levels for learning are low if perceived purpose is not there. Teachers may utilize deductive methods to assist students to perceive purpose in learning. Thus, the teacher may explain the value of new content to be presented to students. Induction may also be used as a means of guiding students to perceive value in learning new facts, concepts, and generalizations in on-going lessons and units. A series of questions asked of students can lead them to accept reasons for learning vital subject matter. Rural school students need to perceive purpose or reasons for achieving objectives in the curriculum.

Fourthly, balance in the curriculum needs to be emphasized. With balance in the curriculum, students need to achieve understandings, skills, and attitudinal goals. Achieving understandings objectives is vital, but not adequate. Achieving facts, concepts, and generalizations emphasized understandings objectives. Skills objectives are also significant in the curriculum. Skills objectives stress listening, speaking, reading, writing, critical and creative thinking, as well as problem solving. The third category of objectives which are attitudinal if achieved by students assists in attaining understandings and skills objectives. Students in rural schools should experience balance among objectives in the curriculum.

Fifthly, students need to experience success in school. New objectives need to be attained by students, but satisfaction in goal attainment must be in evidence. If objectives are too complex to achieve, failure in learning tends to be in evidence. Conversely, with excessively easy objectives for learners to attain, boredom and a lack of challenge may be an end result. Rural school students must achieve new objectives, but success in goal attainment is in evidence.

Philosophy of Teaching the Rural Student

Diverse philosophies of teaching may be utilized by the teacher to provide for individual differences among students.

One philosophical school of thought emphasizes problem solving objectives for students in the curriculum. To become good problem solvers later in society, students need to engage in solving life-like problems in school. Society should not be separated from school, when emphasizing a problem solving philosophy.

Flexible steps of problem solving include:

1. Identification of the problem.
2. Gather data or information to solve the problem.
3. Develop a hypothesis which is tentative and not an absolute.
4. Test the hypothesis.
5. Revise or refute the hypothesis.

To provide for individual differences, teachers need to provide ample opportunities for problem solving experiences in the curriculum. Rural school students need to become good problem solvers.

A second philosophy in teaching emphasizes a subject centred curriculum. Major materials to use in a subject centred curriculum include quality textbooks and workbooks, worksheets, and selected audio visual materials to clarify ideas. Intellectual development is the major objective in a subject centred curriculum. Relevant discussions, oral and written reports, as well as other activities involving higher levels of cognition are important to emphasize in a subject centred curriculum. To develop well intellectually, students need to achieve proficiently in abstract learnings. The finite person in a quality subject centred curriculum reaches toward the infinite. Thus, from a more limited being, one becomes increasingly unlimited or infinite. Mind is real and needs development, encouragement, and attainment.

Relevant, dynamic ideas need to be achieved by learners in all curriculum areas. A worthwhile, demanding subject centred curriculum which provides for individual differences needs to be in the offing. Idealism then emphasizes an idea centred curriculum. Rural school students need to attain subject matter learnings which prepare them for the future. The content learned must prepare the rural school student to live effectively in the world of work and as a future citizen in society.

A third philosophy of education entitled realism emphasizes that one can know the real world as it truly is in and of itself. A replica or duplicate of actual reality can then be known. Behaviourally stated objectives and their implementation emphasize that students either attain or do not attain each end as they are stressed in teaching-learning situations. These measurably stated ends are highly precise. Either a student has or has not attained a specific objective as it is being emphasized in ongoing lessons or units.

Since realism stressed the utilization of behaviourally stated objectives, each student needs to attain as many of these precise ends as possible. One can then measure with precision student achievement in the curriculum. Rural school students need to achieve optimally to prepare them adequately presently for school as well as for the future in society.

Existentialism, as a fourth philosophy of education, stresses decision making by students. Each student needs to be involved in selecting objectives, learning opportunities, and appraisal procedures.

One model in emphasizing existentialism pertains to the utilization of learning centres in the classroom. More tasks or learning opportunities need to be available than what any student can complete. The student then selects the centre and the task to complete. An open-ended curriculum is in evidence. Sequential tasks are selected by each student which emphasize a psychological curriculum. Time on task is highly important. The teacher monitors, stimulates, and encourages student progress. He/she does not lecture, not take a central position in the classroom. Rather, the focal point is the student. The student is to learn, accomplish, achieve, and make decisions. He/she is an active, not a passive, participant in the curriculum. Individual tasks or committee endeavours may be selected for participation by the student. The rural school student needs ample opportunities to make worthwhile choices and decisions.

In Summary

The best of objectives, learning opportunities, and appraisal procedures need to be implemented for rural school students. These students, in many cases, will seek jobs, occupations, and professions as adults in urban areas. Rural school students presently need a curriculum which will assist to achieve optimally in school and in society.

To achieve in an optimal manner, rural school students need to:

1. Develop interest in the curriculum.
2. Attach meaning to ongoing lessons and units.
3. Perceive purpose or reasons for learning.
4. Experience balance among understandings, skills, and attitudinal objectives.
5. Feel successful in teaching-learning situations.

From diverse points of view in the philosophy of education emphasized in teaching, rural school students need to:

1. Become proficient in problem solving. Life in society demands that each person be able to solve personal and social problems.
2. Develop proficiency in abstract academic knowledge. As students go through the diverse levels of schooling,

content emphasized becomes increasingly subject centred and abstract. Mental development of the learner is of utmost importance, as is stressed by idealism.

3. Attain vital, not trivial, in terms of achieving specific, measurably stated objectives, as advocated by realism.
4. Learn to make quality moral choices and decisions as advocated by existentialism.

6

School Administration and the Curriculum

The role of the administrator in the school curriculum has not been clearly defined. Numerous manuscripts published in professional journals, as well as textbooks in school administration, have attempted to pinpoint definite roles that an administrator should perform. However, there is a lack of agreement as to what these roles are or should be.

Roles of the Administrator in the School Setting

The school administrator should provide leadership in guiding teachers in the selection of goals for students to attain. The goals may be open-ended or general in nature. The goals can also be precise and specific. Thus, learner achievement may be measured against the measurable objectives.

The administrator needs to be knowledgeable about objectives in different curriculum areas in order to provide quality leadership. Opposite would be where the blind lead the blind in not knowing which objectives to stress in teaching–learning situations.

Goals and objectives selected should:

1. be relevant for students to achieve;
2. provide for diverse capacity and achievement levels of learners;

3. stimulate interest in learning;
4. guide in establishing purpose or reasons for participating in ongoing activities and experiences.

The above-named criteria provide broad guidelines in developing the curriculum. Even for general objectives, the goals need to be stated in a manner which provide direction in terms of which understandings, skills, and attitudes will be stressed. Thus, the following are general goals but they do indicate *what* will be taught:

To develop within the pupil:

1. an understanding that each paragraph needs to possess coherence of ideas;
2. skill to read content critically in separating facts from opinions, accurate statements from inaccurate content, as well as factual knowledge versus fantasy;
3. an attitude of wanting to learn more about the unit presently being emphasized in the curriculum.

Each of the above general objectives does give guidance to the teacher in emphasizing *what* will be taught, such as in general objective number one—pupils after teaching has occurred will attach meaning to *coherence* of ideas in a paragraph, as distinguished from other kinds or types of learning:

A school or school system may wish to emphasize specific objectives in ongoing units of study. Thus, after instruction, it can be determined if students have or have not achieved an objective. The following emphasize precise, measurable ends:

1. Given an editorial, the student will read the content and list two facts and two options.
2. Given a set of scrambled sentences, the student will arrange the sentences so that proper *sequence* is in evidence.

The administrator then has an important responsibility in providing leadership to improve the quality of objectives in the school curriculum.

Administrative guidance is also needed in emphasizing *process* goals when working in the area of curriculum improvement. For any committee to function well and come up with the best end results possible, teachers and the administrator need to:

1. stay on the topic being pursued. Digressing from the topic wastes time and energy. Teacher's and administrator's time is valuable;
2. seek input from all involved. If selected participants do not contribute within the committee, the end product then does not represent the thinking of all members. There are administrators who are very weak indeed in securing participation of all participants in a committee;
3. respect ideas from all participants. If content presented by a committee member is not respected, the involved person generally will refrain from participation in committee endeavours. Too frequently, the game of politics is played by administrators in determining whose ideas will/will not be respected;
4. clarify ideas presented. A committee must be certain that ideas presented are understood clearly. Ambiguous concepts and vague generalizations must be avoided by committee members.

It is difficult to be a quality leader in guiding discussions within a group setting. A polished leader having no other guidelines to present in committee work hardly will suffice. The "smooth television personality" with few other assets is not able to provide leadership in improving the curriculum.

A second task for administrators is to stimulate teachers to select learning activities in guiding students to achieve worthwhile objectives. The chosen activities must provide for diverse learning styles of individual pupils. Each student has much worth and needs to achieve in an optimal manner. The focal point of public schools is to assist pupils to learn as much as individual capabilities permit. Public schools do not exist to have administrators receive high salaries or prestige. Rather, students need to achieve in order that they may become creative beings attaining self-realization.

Frequently, terms such as the following, are thrown around by national study groups advocating change and reform in education:

1. *Time on task*. It almost sounds as if the students are like a machine in that pupils are able to study continuously and not emphasize human traits. The time on task beliefs state that students learn more if they keep studying and achieve desired objectives. "Time on task" really does not say anything worth-while. Common knowledge is involved in stating that a student achieves more, if he/she stays on the topic being pursued. A more worthwhile facet of the phenomena time on task would be in finding out *how* teachers can improve student's involvement pertaining to the subject matter being learned.

   A student, however, is not a machine in being able to absorb more and more content from diverse academic areas. Rather, the pupil is a human being with feelings, needs, wants, and attitudes. Thus, the affective dimension of the student needs to be fulfilled. The learner experiences feelings of fatigue, joy, contentment, as well as disappointment.

2. *Basic skills*. Too frequently in news reports, the concept *basic skills* is mentioned and elaborated upon. It is stated generally that skills can be identified which all students need to master. These are basic or essential skills. First of all, it probably is impossible to select skills that *all* pupils should learn. Students are individuals and do not require the same abilities for all learners. Even in the area of reading it is uncertain as to which skills any one learner needs in order to read proficiently. Some need more phonics than others. Selected readers may learn to read well utilizing the whole word method rather than phonetic analysis. In teaching, educators deal with individuals and not with groups or mass numbers of individuals. Students are human beings and not machines. They 'master' a skill and may forget it a short time later.

3. *Mastery learning*. No doubt, politics was involved when the concept of mastery learning came into being in education. In learning skills, as was stated previously, it may appear to the teacher that a skill, such as in using guide words in a dictionary, is known or mastered. It may

be that a few minutes later that the pupil has forgotten completely what is meant by guide words, let alone using the concept. Mastery learning sounds good, but educators and lay people need to understand the processes of learning more effectively.

4. *Competency based instruction*. This concept merely emphasizes teachers teaching toward measurably stated objectives previously identified. The precise objectives may have been carefully or carelessly identified. After teaching, the teacher may measure if a pupil has/has not attained the precise objectives. The term *competency based* is greatly inflated in its value. It almost sounds as if other methods of teaching deemphasize competency models.

Administrators need to encourage teachers to utilize a variety of activities including:

1. textbooks, workbooks, encyclopedias, and other reading materials;
2. audio-visual materials (films, filmstrips, slides, pictures, transparencies, study prints, excursions, as well as services of quality resource personnel;
3. computer assisted instruction (CAI) as well as using programmed textbooks for learners.

A variety of learning activities should not be emphasized for the sake of doing so. Rather, the diverse kinds of materials utilized in teaching assist students individually to achieve as much possible.

A third task for administrators is to assist teachers to develop a quality system of evaluating student progress. Evaluation is done to determine how much each pupil has learned. The teacher must know if pupils are learning as much as individual capacities and abilities permit. Students must be challenged to make as much progress as possible. But, it must be remembered that administrators and teachers should not have students attempt to learn that which is too complex and too difficult. Trivia and the irrelevant need to be culled from situations.

Now, back to the specific topic of evaluation. When student progress is being appraised, academic, social, emotional, and moral achievement needs to be noticed. Proper physical development also is significant for each student. Academic achievement alone should not be emphasized. But, intellectual achievement is highly important along with social growth, such as students learning to get along well with each others in an effective manner. Just think of how damaging it would be to the learner to do well in academic learnings only and fail miserably in dealing harmoniously with other human beings. Or, how terrible it would be to achieve extremely well in the academic subject matter areas and yet lack appropriate moral guidelines which provide direction and purpose in life. Too frequently, national study groups have advocated excellence in education. Excellence according to these study groups means achieving extremely well in the academic domain only. The authors would like to warn against this line of thinking. For example, supposing that a student would achieve well in subject matter areas only and lack proper emotional achievement. After all, the emotions (feelings, values, and beliefs) of a person are highly significant. Negative feelings continuously exhibited by any one person can make life very unpleasant for others in society as well as for the involved person.

Further Cautions on Recommendations

There certainly are an excess number of recommendations coming out on how to improve the public schools. However, there is little agreement on how to improve the public school curriculum. One must issue cautions on the following:

1. an excess amount of faith placed upon test results to notice student progress. Statewide tests cost much money in their development and use. Could the money be utilized more effectively in other ways, such as buying updated textbooks and other teaching materials? It takes *much* time for teachers to be secretaries and record test results of students. Here, the time of the teacher could be utilized much more wisely by preparing for and implementing quality plans for teaching;
2. advocating developing better textbooks than are presently on the market. Too frequently, the lay public believes the more difficult it is for pupils such as printed content in textbooks, the better it is for learners. The authors would caution against the concept *the more complex something is,*

the better. Better it would be if the lay public and educators advocate helping each student achieve as much as possible, but not frustrate students with unattainable goals;

3. "high expectancies for students." The authors would caution against parents, and administrators having expectancies which are unattainable for students. The dropout rate of pupils from schools might then be extremely high. Situations such as these would not solve problems pertaining to the student's individual future;

4. strong business-school partnerships. The business world represents the private sector which President Reagan holds in extremely high esteem. The public schools represent the public sector which cannot and must not emphasize the profit motive. Schools exist to aid each pupil to achieve as much as possible;

   Assistance the business world could provide to the public schools is to develop a quality curriculum for each learner. The business world must realize that they can learn much from the public schools. For example, the public schools must accept each student regardless of the quality involved. They (the schools) cannot shut down and move away when undesirable students are in the offing. Businesses, however, may close their doors and move to a foreign nation where cheaper labour can be secured in order to stay solvent or even to secure greater profits;

5. schools must give students the basic skills in order that the latter may get a job. The certainly is an unintelligent statement that a United States senator made. First of all, no one can *give* an education to others. Each must reach out and learn. If skills could be given, the authors would like to have those abilities possessed by leading scientists. Secondly, who can play the role of God to know which skills any one person might need in the future?

6. the principal needs to be a strong leader in the school due to "as the administrator is in his/her leadership—so is the achievement of students within the school." The above statement gives administrators an almost blank check to be dictators in improving the curriculum. Certainly, an

administrator has a vital role to improve the curriculum. However, a hierarchical structure whereby *relevancy* in ideas moves only in the direction from the administrator to teachers is not recommended. Today's teachers is well educated, and, no doubt, does well in coping with negative situations, such as low salaries, unfortunate home environments of students, inadequate instructional materials in schools to provide for individual differences, and the ever present budget cutter on local school boards. Thus, administrators and teachers cooperatively need develop a curriculum which truly assists each pupil to achieve as much as abilities will permit;

7. cost/benefit analysis is the key to effective practices in education. Thus, the cost of pupils' attaining each measurable objective is computed. However, the attained objective may represent trivia. There are learnings attained which are highly significant and not measurable, such as creative thinking. Being able to think creatively has certainly changed society and made for positive improvements;
8. changes need to be made quickly in education. No statement is ever made in which direction(s) the modifications should go. The lay public and selected educators look to the past for goals and emphasize the tried and true basics to be emphasized in the school curriculum. Many educators, however, look toward to the future in ascertaining objectives for student attainment. These goals emphasize a comprehensive curriculum, much broader than the basics (reading, writing, and arithmetic).

The writers wonder why major changes are not emphasized and made in the legal and the medical professions. Also, the financial institutions, the home, and elected officials need to appraise themselves and come up with desired changes to benefit human beings in society.

In Closing

Teachers, supervisors, and parents need to establish worthwhile objectives for students to achieve. The goals selected need to be relevant and feasible for students to realize. Each student needs to achieve in an optimal manner.

REFERENCES

Cruickshank, Donald R. *Teaching is Tough*. Englewood Cliffs, New Jersey: Prentice-Hall, Inc., 1980.

Henson, Kenneth T. *Secondary Teaching Methods*. Lexington, Massachusetts: D.C. Heath and Company, 1981.

Joyce, Bruce, and Marsha Weil. *Models of Teaching*. Third edition. Englewood Cliffs, New Jersey: Prentice-Hall, Inc., 1986.

Joyce, Bruce, et al. *The Structure of School Improvement*. New York: Longmans, 1983.

National Society for the Study of Education. *Staff Development*, Part II. Chicago, Illinois: The Society, 1983.

National Society for the Study of Education. *The Humanities in Precollegiate Education*, Part II. Chicago, Illinois: The Society, 1984.

National Society for the Study of Education. *Becoming Readers in a Complex Society*, Part I. Chicago, Illinois: The Society, 1984.

National Society for the Study of Education. *Education in School and Non-School Settings*, Part I. Chicago, Illinois: The Society, 1985.

tional Society for the Study of Education. *The Ecology of School Renewal*, Part I. Chicago, Illinois: The Society, 1987.

National Society for the Study of Education. *Society as Education in an Age of Transition*, Part II. Chicago, Illinois: The Society, 1987.

7

Student Motivation in Reading

Motivation is a rather persistent problem in guiding students to read well. If a student lacks motivation, a low energy level will be available in learning to read. Through motivation, a learner is encouraged to achieve definite goals in reading. Persistence is there to aid students in goal attainment with adequately motivated behaviour.

Why Motivation is Important?

Students who lack motivation do not pay adequate attention to ongoing learning opportunities. Chances to learn then are minimized. Later on, these students need to make up deficiencies from the lost opportunities to learn. If a student does not concentrate and focus upon new words in reading on the chalkboard introduced by the teacher, the chances are these words will not be identified while reading the related content. The learner must put forth effort and energy to view each word carefully. Attempts need to be made by involved students to retain the correct identification of the new words. Otherwise, new learnings will be forgotten before their implementation in reading required subject matter. It is the student that must do the learning and, in this case, learn to identify words correctly, as they are being introduced by the teacher of reading. Adequate motivation on the part of the learner is necessary to attend to and retain identification of new words introduced by the teacher.

Attention and retention by the student is important in recognizing new words whether the approach is through phonics instruction, syllabication, structural analysis, configuration clues, use of picture clues, or identification of words through contextual situations.

Why Motivation is Lacking?

Numerous reasons are given for students lacking motivation. Frequently, teachers are blamed for learners not being motivated due to poor teaching methods. This may be one reason. Teachers need to feel challenge covering the subject matter being taught. *Enthusiasm* of teachers might be reflected within learners. Thus, a teacher who enthusiastically tells learners what he/she has read and demonstrates interest in reading content, as well as in teaching reading to each student, may well encourage the latter to read proficiently. Certainly, a motivated teacher teaching students to read critically and creatively should have the enthusiasm reflected within learners.

There are numerous other reasons for students lacking motivation in reading. A variety of reading materials, including textbooks, library books, and other print materials must be available for learners to provide for *individual differences*. It certainly is not motivating for learners if the subject matter read is too complex or excessively easy. Each student needs to be ready for reading specific subject matter. Readiness factors to motivate students to read include having ample opportunities to see new words in print, attach meaning to each new word, have adequate background information, as well as have a purpose (reason) to read, prior to reading the involved subject matter. Motivation to read may be lacking due to students lacking readiness factors.

Subject matter to be read should be of *interest* to students. A lack of interesting reading materials can make for inappropriate motivation. With interest in subject matter being read, students possess a high energy level for reading. Motivation is inherent when each student is interested in reading the involved subject matter.

Reading teachers must use a *variety* of stimulating methods in teaching students. To learn inductively on the part of students, the teacher needs to ask challenging questions covering content read.

Each question needs to be on the understanding level of students. Questions to motivate students need to lead to higher levels of thinking, such as the levels of analysis (separating facts from opinions, fantasy from reality, accurate from inaccurate content, as well as detecting bias, glittering generalities, and card stacking), synthesis (hypothesizing), and evaluation (appraising subject matter read in terms of quality criteria).

Quality deductive methods to motivate student behaviour may emphasize a teacher modelling analysis, synthesis, and evaluation in reading. Motivated students apply what has been learned pertaining to higher levels of cognition.

Problem solving methods should also be utilized to stimulate student reading. Here, students with teacher guidance identify stimulating problems or broad questions. Information is gathered through reading and the use of audiovisual materials. A hypothesis is tested in action and revised if necessary. Problem solving methods are good to utilize when students select interesting problems pertaining to subject matter read. A variety of reading materials and non-reading activities assist in data gathering, as well as in checking hypothesis. Critical and creative thinking are emphasized in true problem solving experiences. Problems identified are new to involved students. Challenge is involved in choosing learning opportunities to solve the identified problems. If the same methods are utilized continuously, students will tend to dislike reading. Problems identified by students with teacher guidance integrate interest with effort. Interest provides for effort in learning. Motivation is then present.

Balance among cognitive, affective, and psychomotor objectives should be emphasized in teaching reading. A single domain of objectives, such as cognitive, is not adequate. The development of the intellect (cognition) is significant in the teaching of reading. Students then need to learn to achieve skills in reading to follow directions, skim, or scan, develop sequence in ideas, as well as achieve main ideas and generalization. Analyzing what has been read and achieving unique ideas covering subject matter ideas are further relevant cognitive goals. Affective objectives, however, stimulate students to do well in the cognitive domain.

The affective dimension of objectives is equally important as compared to the cognitive domain. With desirable affective objectives, students learn to select and enjoy quality literature. When ready, a learner then enjoys characterization, setting, plot, irony, and theme of literature read. An individualized reading programme needs to be in evidence in which the student feels motivated by selecting the title and achievement level of the library book. Hopefully, challenging library books will be selected by the learner. The teacher in a conference with the student needs to encourage, not force, increased interest in reading. Fascinating questions raised by the teacher and the student can be discussed within the conference setting. Evaluation of the success of each conference would emphasize students doing more reading and appreciating subject matter content.

The psychomotor level of objectives should receive adequate attention in the reading curriculum to motivate student learning. With psychomotor goals, students develop proficiency in using the gross and finer muscles, as well as skill in eye-hand coordination. Numerous fascinating learning opportunities can be stressed by the teacher in the psychomotor domain. Thus, after reading content from basal textbooks or through an individualized reading programme, learners may complete stimulating projects to reveal comprehension. These projects include:

1. developing a mural or pencil sketching;
2. making a diorama;
3. creating a pantomime or creative dramatics presentation;
4. completing a movie set, showing illustrated scenes of subject matter read;
5. writing a different beginning or ending for the story with accompanying illustrations;
6. constructing a model relating directly to ideas contained in a story or reading selection.

Teachers of reading then need to have students attain balance among cognitive, affective, and psychomotor objectives. Each objective needs to stress encouragement and motivation for learning.

Students may lack motivation in reading due to a lack of meaningful learning. The reader needs to relate the self to the selection being read. The reading teacher must make certain that students understand subject matter. Students who do not read well enough to benefit from the reading of the textbook need assistance. A good reader could orally read the contents to the disabled reader as the latter follows along in his/her book. If not overdone as a method, this can be challenging to both students. The disabled reader can then learn to identify words in the process as well as listen to the ideas read. Attaching meaning to the subject matter listened to is then possible. Motivation to read new materials may be a relevant end result. Gifted/talented readers need to read challenging materials; otherwise a lack of meaning is not possible when subject matter is boring and lacks maturity. These learners must be assisted to achieve optimally. This will be well above the grade level they are presently in. If a student with eighth or ninth grade reading abilities is asked to utilize textbooks written for fifth graders, it is no wonder that motivation to read is lacking. Or a fifth grader, reading on the second grade level, will lack motivation to read content written for average achievers in grade five.

The key to successful reading achievement of students is to match their present level of attainment with materials of instruction that are meaningful and possess challenge.

Recommendations to Improve the Reading Curriculum

Numerous recommendations have been made by experts to improve reading skills on the part of students. The writers would like to recommend definite quality criteria to assist students to achieve more optimally in reading.

First of all, with the accountability movement in vogue, basic essential skills for students have been identified on the state or local school level. These skills are generally listed as behaviourally stated objectives. The reading curriculum then becomes fragmented. Each student needs to attain these sequential precise ends. Too much time by the reading teacher needs to be spent on having learners achieve each behaviourally stated objective. Little time may be available to have students read subject matter in a holistic approach. Learning of isolated skills becomes relevant, rather than reading sequential ideas in order to learn. Certainly, comprehension of quality literature must be the end result, rather than acquiring isolate 1 reading skills. Enjoying literature read should be a true motivator for students.

Secondly, the writers recommend that students have a greater voice in determining which sources to read from and which problem areas to solve, involving the processes of reading. Student-teacher planning of goals, experiences, and appraisal procedures, emphasize a sound philosophy of education. Interest of student provides for effort in learning. Motivation is then present in the learning opportunities.

Thirdly, motivated, well educated and trained teachers should be able to make good decisions in terms of providing for individual differences in reading. With state mandated objectives or local district instructional management systems (IMS), decision making by the reading teacher is minimized. Certainly, a quality motivated teacher should be able to determine scope and sequence better than can be done on the state or district-wide level. Each teacher, regardless of age level of students taught or academic area taught, must be a teacher of reading. The making of decisions by the teacher may become a motivator in and of itself. This enthusiasm is reflected within learners.

Fourthly, state certification departments need to require in teacher preparation programmes that all prospective teachers have adequate course work in the teaching of reading. Schools of education preparing teachers need to be certain that all have demonstrated proficiency in the teaching of reading. Teachers need to possess adequate knowledge and skill in teaching word recognition techniques and diverse kinds of comprehension skills to develop within students. A love for the teaching of reading and an ability to motivate students is a must in teacher education programmes.

Fifthly, teachers need to stimulate students to enjoy and appreciate reading. It is a blessing to be a good reader. Non-readers or those limited in the ability to read suffer grave consequences in society. The level of job attainment is lowered if an adult cannot read at a required proficient level. Enjoyment of life is minimized due to not possessing needed skills in reading. Too frequently, the student and parents do not appreciate the opportunities to learn. Opportunities to learn involve the skill of reading.

Sixthly, teachers need to stimulate students to move to higher cognition levels, as compared to rote learning and drill experiences.

Students should experience needed drill and practice in reading subject matter. However, life itself demands that learners be skillful in problem solving situations. Reading of content provides opportunities to students with teacher assistance to identify vital problems, gather related data and achieve answers to each problem. The ability to motivate students to higher levels of cognition is a must for the teacher.

Seventhly, students should experience life vicariously. It is impossible to experience, in many situations, desirable situations in life. Through reading or vicariously, learners may experience what is good, true, and beautiful. Undesirable situations in life are costly to experience directly. With vicarious experiences in reading, what is undesirable can be experienced in a relatively harmless manner. Learners need to be motivated to experience life vicariously.

In closing, a quality reading curriculum needs much planning. Careful attention to vital objectives, relevant learning opportunities to read, and important evaluation procedures can truly make for a quality reading curriculum. Hopefully, students will be motivated to read with quality planning in evidence from the teacher.

REFERENCES

Alexander, J. Estill (Editor). *Teaching Reading*. Second edition. Boston: Little, Brown and Company, 1983.

Davis, Gary A. *Educational Psychology*. New York: Random House, 1983.

Harris Albert, and Edward Sipay. *How to Increase Reading Ability*. Eighth edition. New York: Longman, Inc., 1985.

Ringler, Lenore H., and Carol K. Weber. *A Language-Thinking Approach to Reading*. New York: Harcourt Brace Jovanovich, 1984.

Rubin, Dorothy. *Diagnosis and Correction in Reading Instruction*. New York: Holt, Rinehart and Winston, 1982.

8

Priorities in the Social Studies

There are numerous articles and textbooks written on improving the teaching of the social studies. Thus, many issues are in evidence in objectives, learning activities, subject matter, and appraisal procedures in the social studies area.

Analyzing Recommendations in Teaching the Social Studies

An increased number of states mandate the use of precise objectives in teaching. Thus, on the local school system level, measurably stated objectives are identified by social studies teachers and supervisors. Students are to attain these ends as a result of teaching. The school district also develops tests for students to take to reveal if the specific objectives have been achieved. Observable results are then secured from students. Basically, slow, average, and fast learners can attain the same objectives. However, slower students need more assistance to achieve goals.

Behaviourism, as a psychology of learning, is involved in social studies teachers selecting measurable objectives for students to achieve.

There are selected criticisms of behaviourism and its use in the social studies. Students have their own desired goals to achieve. These goals may emphasize questions which learners raise in ongoing units and study. Students then desire to discuss answers to purposeful questions and problems. Objectives developed prior to instruction, such as in behaviourism, omit the concept of student-teacher planning.

Secondly, the order of emphasizing the precise objectives in teaching is determined by the social studies teacher. There are selected educators who believe that sequence resides within the student and not in predetermined measurably stated objectives. It is the student then who needs to be involved in determining the order of objectives.

Thirdly, precise objectives selected for student attainment may emphasize trivia. Critical and creative thinking as well as problem solving are difficult goals to state in precise terms. Thus, higher levels of thinking are omitted from the social studies curriculum.

Advocates of specific objectives favour clarity of ends to stress in teaching. With measurably stated objectives, there is little or no disagreement in meaning of what students are to learn. Clearly stated objectives are salient to a behaviourist, otherwise vagueness exists in stating content that students are to attain.

Furthermore, if subject matter is carefully identified prior to instruction, trivia will be avoided as a content for learners to acquire. Careful consideration needs to be given to subject matter selected for students to acquire. The subject matter chosen by social studies teachers and supervisors needs to be incorporated into the specific objectives to be emphasized in the curriculum.

An adequate number of objectives needs to be in the offing for pupils so that success in achievement is enhanced. If students experience difficulties between achieving objectives one and two, additional ends can be placed between these two goals of instruction.

Behaviourists believe it is easier to select learning activities if the objectives are stated in a precise, specific manner. The learning activities chosen, be it reading and/or audio-visual aids, should help students to attain one or more specific objectives. It might be that a single filmstrip, properly introduced to students, guides students to achieve one objective. At other times a single learning activity will guide students to attain two or more objectives.

Behaviourists also advocate that evaluation procedures can be highly reliable if the appraisal procedures utilized measures learner progress against the stated objective. The concept of reliability is highly significant when thinking of methods of evaluating student progress in the social studies.

An eclectic approach in teaching social studies would emphasize using both measurably stated as well as general objectives that are more open ended in ongoing lessons and units of instruction.

A second issue in teaching social studies emphasizes a state mandate versus a locally developed curriculum. Diverse states have definitely become increasingly involved in determining criteria for local school districts to follow. Selected states mandate the use of measurably stated objectives for schools to follow. Other states permit local districts to decide upon the use or non-use of measurably stated objectives. If measurably stated objectives are stressed, then mastery learning, instructional management systems (IMS), or criterion referenced testing (CRT) is emphasized in teaching and learning situations.

Further issues in a state mandated social studies curriculum stresses the selection of subject matter to be taught to students. A state might then have subject matter specialists in the academic disciplines of history, geography, political science, economics, anthropology and sociology determine content for learners to acquire. Advocates of academic experts deciding upon facts, concepts, and generalizations that students need to acquire believe that vital content would then be in evidence in the social studies. Trivia might then be minimized. Whichever content is selected on the state level would be mandated for learner acquisition. Each social studies teacher then needs to select methods and materials in teaching students to insure optimal progress.

Toward the other end of the continuum, a local school district could identify salient understandings for students to attain. The social studies teachers must determine means of assisting learners to attain the vital subject matter. There would be adequate latitude for the social studies teacher personally to select facts, concepts, and generalizations for learner attainment. In a state mandated curriculum of subject matter in the social studies, the local teacher and / or school district may supplement that which the state requires of all students.

An eclectic approach could well emphasize state mandated subject matter for student attainment, as well as the school district and individual social studies teachers choose significant facts, concepts, and generalizations to emphasize in ongoing lessons and units.

A third issue in the social studies curriculum pertains to who should be involved in appraising student achievement. States individually may develop and mandate that all learners complete tests written by measurement specialists. This could well be a criterion referenced test (CRT) in which social studies teachers receive from the state level precise, measurable objectives that students need to achieve in order to do well on the mandated CRT. Or, the state may legislate that all students therein take a standardized, norm referenced test. Comparisons may be made of one school district against another in determining which school system, school building, or individual classroom of students exhibited the highest average test scores in the CRT or the norm referenced test.

Traditionally, each social studies teacher has written tests (true-false, multiple choice, matching, completion, and essay) for students to reveal their level of understanding pertaining to subject matter learned. Valid and reliable teacher written test items could measure effectively what students have learned.

An eclectic approach in appraisal procedures would emphasize state mandated tests, as well as districtwide, and teacher written test items to ascertain what each student has achieved.

A fourth issue in teaching social studies involves method of teaching. Should students largely acquire subject matter inductively or deductively? In an inductive approach, the social studies teacher needs to be a good asker of questions to lead students to achieve significant generalizations. Or, the teacher needs to have students identify problems, gather data, develop hypotheses, test each hypothesis, and revise if needed. Students should be guided to discover and to find information relative to the solving of problems.

Somewhat toward the other end of the continuum is a deductive method of teaching. With deduction, the social studies teacher explains in a meaningful manner generalizations of vital subject matter to learners. Students then need to study and give examples of each generalization taught. The social studies teacher may also provide specific instances related directly to the generalization emphasized by the teacher. Concrete, semi-concrete, and abstract experiences may be utilized in deductive thinking.

Most social studies teachers are eclectic in emphasizing both inductive as well as deductive methods of teaching.

A fifth issue emphasizes depth versus survey methods of teaching. Depth teaching is superior to survey means. With depth teaching, the social studies teacher takes ample time with quality learning activities to assist students to learn much pertaining to each fact, concept, and generalization being taught. Attempting to cover much ground and subject matter in a short period of time is not advocated in depth teaching.

Survey means of teaching stress, covering comprehensive subject matter in a relatively short time devoted to instruction. Realia, iconic, and symbolic learnings may be implemented in either depth or survey approaches of teaching and learning.

There are reasons why survey methods of instruction are utilized. A social studies teacher could not teach each vital fact, concept, and generalization in depth. There is inadequate time to do so. Thus, the teacher must decide how much emphasis in each social studies unit should be depth and how much survey teaching pertaining to each cognitive, affective, and psychomotor objective.

A sixth issue emphasizes the degree that a subject centred social studies curriculum should be in emphasis as compared to activity centred units of study. A subject matter approach would emphasize rather heavy use of social studies textbooks, workbooks, and worksheets. A few audio-visual aids need utilization and clarify content being studied.

An activity centred procedure in ongoing units would emphasize the heavy utilization of audio-visual materials, construction and dramatic experiences, music and rhythmic activities, simulations, and problem solving. The student is considered an active, not a passive, being in the social studies.

An eclectic social studies teacher would tend to emphasize both subject matter and project approaches in teaching. An important ingredient would be to provide for fast, average, and slow learners in the curriculum. Providing for individual differences is more salient than the debate pertaining to a subject as compared to activity centred methods of teaching.

A seventh issue pertains to the use of microcomputers in the social studies. How much use should be made of computer technology? There are numerous reasons given for emphasizing microcomputer instruction? These include:

1. individual differences can be more adequately provided for with appropriate software;
2. effective sequence is in evidence with quality software;
3. variety in learning opportunities is stressed;
4. drill and practice, tutorial, simulation, games, diagnosis and remediation, as well as computer managed instruction (CMI) to score tests is possible;
5. computers are patient in assisting students again and again in learning.

The writers have visited with many classroom teachers to have them indicate the lack of microcomputer use in the social studies. The reasons given for non-use of microcomputers includes:

1. software is not available which relates directly to ongoing lessons and units;
2. an inadequate number of microcomputers are available to provide any type of sequential learning for students;
3. available software is not on the present achievement levels of students;
4. the order of content presented does not provide for individual students.

Once adequate numbers of microcomputers and software are available, the social studies teacher needs to:

1. determine the degree in which technology will be utilized to assist learner optimal progress;
2. assist students to achieve sequentially in terms of improved software;

3. aid learners to attach meaning to content learned utilizing software and microcomputers;
4. help students of diverse achievement levels learn as much as possible;
5. stimulate interest in learning from various technologies of instruction.

In Conclusion

There are numerous issues needing resolving in the social studies curriculum. These issues include:

1. state mandated versus local decisions made in the teaching of social studies;
2. emphasis upon inductive as compared to deductive methods of teaching;
3. depth versus survey approaches in ongoing units and lessons;
4. a subject centred versus an activity centred curriculum;
5. degrees of microcomputer and software use in the social studies.

Students individually need to achieve optimally. There are many social problems to solve on the planet earth. These problems include:

1. pollution in the environment;
2. poverty and unemployment;
3. wars and rumours of wars;
4. disease prevention and control;
5. racial discrimination;
6. lack of opportunities in life;
7. child and spouse abuse;
8. right of freedom of speech.

The social studies is a highly significant area of the curriculum. It no doubt could be considered the most important academic and curriculum area. If problems in society are not identified and attempts made at finding solutions, other facets of life cannot be utilized to benefit the human condition.

9

Psychology in Teaching Mathematics

Numerous reputable psychologies are provided to assist mathematics teachers to guide each student to achieve optimally. The teacher of mathematics should study the diverse psychologies of education to implement the best teaching strategy possible. The lay public focuses on student achievement in the 3 r's or basics. Mathematics represents a highly salient basic. Students need to achieve well in mathematics to do well in school and in society. The societal arena demands mathematics proficiency within students. Learners in school need guidance to fulfill those responsibilities. Teachers need to select objectives, learning opportunities and appraisal procedures which assist each learner to achieve as well as is possible.

- The balance of this paper will emphasize specific psychologies of education, applicable to teaching-learning situations in the classroom.

Behaviourism in the Mathematics Curriculum

Precise, measurably stated objectives and their use is the heart of behaviourism. These objectives are selected prior to their being implemented in the classroom. Generally, no student participation has been emphasized in selecting these goals. Behaviourism can be emphasized with state mandated objectives in terms of core competencies and key skills. On the state level precise measurably stated objectives have been chosen. The department of education of each state selects a cross section of educators within their borders to agree upon the stated ends. The mathematics teacher then plans learning opportunities to have students attain each objectives.

A second example of behaviourism emphasizes instructional management systems (IMS) on the district level. The central office then selects a cross section of teachers within the district to select salient objectives in mathematics. Again, the classroom teacher must emphasize each objective in teaching-learning situations.

The mathematics teacher, without stated mandated objectives or IMS, may write and implement specific ends for student attainment. Teaching strategies need selecting which insures that students attain desired ends.

An early pioneer in measurably stated objectives and their use was B.F. Skinner. Dr. Skinner emphasized programmed learning in either textbook or software form. The ingredients of programmed learning include:

1. sequential items of small amounts of information acquired by students in each step of learning;
2. students responding to a test item, such as a multiple choice item, based on information presented in book or software form;
3. learners receiving feedback based on the response made;
4. reinforcement being rather common with high frequency of correct responses made.

Behaviourism, in its diverse manifestations, emphasizes that a student either does or does not achieve an objective as a result of instruction. If an end is not attained, the mathematics teacher needs to try a different teaching strategy.

Behaviourism appears to be a dominant psychology of education emphasized in the teaching of mathematics. With the popularity of behaviourism, the writers recommend:

1. each obje-tive in mathematics be carefully selected in terms of being useful in school, as well as in society;

2. students achieving success in attaining sequential objectives;
3. a variety of challenging learning opportunities being provided for learners to attain each end;
4. students experiencing meaning, interest, and purpose in achieving desired ends;
5. critical and creative thinking, as well as problem solving, receiving ample attention in the mathematics curriculum;
6. appraisal procedures being varied, valid, and reliable to evaluate learner progress.

Humanism in the Mathematics Curriculum

Humanism, as a psychology of learning, emphasizes students being heavily involved in determining objectives, learning opportunities and evaluation procedures. Each student is guided to attain self realization. The late A.H. Maslow, humanist psychologist, listed five sequential levels for individuals to move through to achieve realization of the self. These include:

(a) assisting students to meet physiological needs, such as adequate food, clothing, and proper shelter;

(b) helping learners to feel safe and secure in their environment;

(c) guiding students in meeting love and belonging needs;

(d) developing situations in which esteem needs of students are being met;

(e) assisting learners to achieve self actualization.

Only after the above sequential needs of students have been met can students achieve optimally, according to humanism, as a psychology of learning. It certainly behooves any school system to meet needs of students in order that increased achievement can be in the offing.

To pinpoint the mathematics curriculum more thoroughly, input from learners in selecting objectives, learning opportunities, and appraisal procedures is highly important. There are several excellent ways of emphasizing humanism in the mathematics curriculum. One plan is to utilize learning centres. More tasks than any one student can complete would be at the diverse centres. Students individually learn to make decisions. They choose which tasks sequentially to complete and which to omit. Each learner then selects what is perceived to be of interest, meaning, and purpose. Students do not need to work on tasks perceived to be of little or no value. Sequence, in selecting ordered tasks, resides within the student. A psychological curriculum is then in evidence. Internally, the student makes choices in terms of tasks in mathematics to pursue.

A second plan of humanism, as a psychology of education, is to use a contract system. In a contract, the student and his/her teacher plan cooperatively specific learning opportunities for the former to complete. There must be considerable input from the student on the contract for humanistic psychology to be in evidence. The date the contract is due must be indicated together with the student and the teacher's signature.

A third plan of humanism is in the offing when the teacher lists, for example, ten activities for students to consider to complete in mathematics. Each student may choose five or more to complete. The student here has input as to what to pursue and what to omit.

Humanism emphasizes a humane mathematics curriculum. Humanness is defined as students being able to decide from among alternatives which learning activities possess value and need to be completed satisfactorily.

The writers, in evaluating humanism, in teaching mathematics recommend that:

1. worthwhile tasks be developed for students to pursue sequentially. Trivia is to be omitted for learners to pursue;
2. students be guided to stay on task and not digress from achieving relevant objectives;
3. tasks be written on diverse levels of achievement to challenge each student to achieve as much as possible.

The Structure of Knowledge

During the 1960s and early 1970s much emphasis was placed upon mathematicians on the higher education level identifying structural ideas for public school students to attain. The structure of knowledge emphasized underlying principles that provided a framework for an academic discipline. Thus, in the academic discipline of mathematics, selected broad generalizations provided a structure for students in ongoing lessons and units. The key ideas then, among others, included the commutative property of addition and multiplication, the distributive property of multiplication over addition, the property of closure, and the identity elements.

The structure of knowledge approach, as identified by Jerome Bruner of Harvard University and his associates emphasized that public school students utilize methods of learning utilized by mathematicians on the higher education level. An inductive procedure is then in evidence. Students are guided by the teacher to learn by discovery in moving from the specific to the general to achieve structural ideas. Materials to use in teaching students to acquire content inductively include inactive (manipulative items), iconic (pictures, drawings, slides and filmstrips emphasizing main ideas), and symbolic (abstract content such as printed words and numerals).

The structure of knowledge approach has much to recommend itself. The writers recommend that:

1. teachers emphasize structural ideas in a spiral curriculum. However, the spiral curriculum should not be excessively repetitious. There is built in review in the structure when these key generalizations receive attention at more complex levels in the mathematics curriculum;
2. induction receive adequate attention in teaching-learning situations. However, continued use of inductive methods are time consuming to use. The mathematics teacher needs to inject meaningful explanations also at definite points in ongoing lessons and units;
3. creative teaching in using diverse methodologies be emphasized thoroughly. Methods and subject matter have to be adjusted to the present achievement level of each student. Students differ from each other in many ways, such as interests, purposes, and present levels of achievement.

Diagnosis in Mathematics

The mathematics teacher must utilize the concept of diagnosis in teaching-learning situations. To diagnose means to pinpoint specific difficulties students experience in computation, concept development and problem solving. Students need assistance to overcome errors made.

Robert Gagné in his book *The Conditions of Learning* (New York: Holt Rinehart and Winston publishers, 1985) advocates a hierarchy of objectives be stated in measurable terms for student attainment. If a learner cannot achieve a specific end, the teacher needs to move to a sequential easier objective. Reversing to easier ends is necessary until the present attainment level of the involved student is found. The last three levels of Gagne's hierarchy are especially important to know when teachers diagnose difficulties students experience in mathematics. The three in sequence are concept learning, rule learning, and problem solving. Thus, if a student cannot solve a problem in mathematics, the teacher needs to assist the former to determine if he/she understands involved rules. For example, if the problem to be solved involves finding the volume of a cylinder, the student must understand the involved formula—$r^2\pi h$. If the learner does not understand the rule to determine the volume of a cylinder, he/she needs assistance in attaching meaning to concepts. The separate concepts are radius, radius times radius, pi, and height. After the concepts have been learned, followed by the student acquiring the rule, the chances are that the problem can be solved in finding the volume of a cylinder.

Diagnosis is involved when the mathematics teacher assists the student to pinpoint specific weaknesses in a lesson or unit. Assistance and guidance needs to be provided to the learner to overcome identified deficiencies. Robert Gagné provides a quality model for mathematics teachers to follow in helping learners to progress sequentially. The diagnosis and remediation concepts in Gagne's hierarchy of objectives can give much help to teachers in guiding each student to attain as much as possible in mathematics.

In using diagnostic-remediation procedures in the teaching of mathematics, the writers recommends that:

1. students attach meaning to each sequential step of learning;

2. learners be assisted to perceive holism and sequence in subject matter learned. Diagnosis is available if a student fails to attach meaning to ongoing rules (generalizations) and concepts in order to solve problems in mathematics.

In Conclusion

Relevant principles of learning from the psychology of education need to be implemented in teaching-learning situations. The teacher of mathematics must assist each student to attain in an optimal manner.

Four schools of thought were discussed in the psychology of education. These were behaviourism, humanism, the structure of knowledge and diagnosis based on a hierarchy of objectives.

The writers recommend that mathematics teachers:

1. implement tenets of behaviourism with its measurably stated objectives. Higher levels of cognition must not be hindered with the use of behaviourism in teaching-learning situations;
2. provide ample opportunities for students to engage in decision making. Learners need to have chances to select sequential learning opportunities, as advocated by humanism;
3. stress the structure of knowledge so that students may perceive that subject matter is related;
4. adequately diagnose and remediate student problems in lessons and units. Students need to perceive mathematics as being holistic and not isolated specifics in diagnostic/ remediation situations.

REFERENCES

Cruickshank, Donald R. *Teaching is Tough*. Englewood Cliffs, New Jersey: Prentice-Hall, Inc., 1980.

Henson, Kenneth T. *Secondary Teaching Methods*. Lexington, Massachusetts: D.C. Heath and Company, 1981.

Joyce, Bruce, and Marsha Weil. *Models of Teaching*. Third edition. Englewood Cliffs, New Jersey: Prentice-Hall, Inc., 1986.

Joyce, Bruce, *et al*. *The Structure of School Improvement*. New York: Longmans, 1983.

National Society for the Study of Education. *Staff Development*, Part II. Chicago, Illinois: The Society, 1983.

National Society for the Study of Education. *The Humanities in Precollegiate Education*, Part II. Chicago, Illinois: The Society, 1984.

National Society for the Study of Education. *Becoming Readers in a Complex Society*, Part I. Chicago, Illinois: The Society, 1984.

National Society for the Study of Education. *Education in School and Non-School Settings*, Part I. Chicago, Illinois: The Society, 1985.

National Society for the Study of Education. *The Ecology of School Renewal*, Part I. Chicago, Illinois: The Society, 1987.

National Society for the Study of Education. *Society as Education in an Age of Transition*, Part II. Chicago, Illinois: The Society, 1987.

10

The Integrated Science Curriculum

In appraising the breadth of the science curriculum, *scope* as a concept becomes significant. Scope attempts to answer the question of *what* should be taught in ongoing lessons and units. Shepherd and Ragan[1] list degrees in which subject matter can be related. They discuss the separate subjects, correlated, fused, and integrated curriculum.

The separate subjects curriculum with its many compartmentalizations of knowledge was prevalent up to the early 1990's. However, leading educators for their day emphasized correlation. Joseph Lancaster[2] and his monitorial system of instruction in 1805, stressed relating reading with spelling and writing. What students learned to read, they should also be able to write, according to Lancaster. He had a carefully written curriculum for each class level of instruction whereby students could be promoted individually from one class level to the next. As was typical for his day, no science was taught in the Lancastrian monitorial system of instruction.

Johann Friederich Pestalozzi[3] (1746-1827), Swiss educator, emphasized object lessons in teaching. Object lessons in science stressed the concrete and the real. Thus, if insects were studied in science, the actual insect was viewed by students to notice the head, thorax and abdomen among other items. Concrete materials formed the basis for discussions in science object lessons.

Johann Friedrich Herbart[4] (1776-1841) strongly advocated correlation in teaching. Herbart's five steps of teaching were:

1. *Preparation*. Here the teacher reviews with pupils previously taught content so that these ideas would be clear and sharp.
2. *Presentation*. New content is taught to students.
3. *Comparison*. The student is assisted to connect or correlate the steps of presentation with that of preparation.
4. *Generalization*. With associations developed the teacher assists students to achieve broad conclusions and summaries of subject matter learned.
5. *Application*. Students use content acquired.

Herbart was strong in emphasizing a correlated curriculum. Too many isolated ideas definitely fragments the curriculum. Subject matter such as that is soon forgotten. Rather, relationship of subject matter taught assists students to retain and remember better, as compared to the separate subjects curriculum.

John Dewey[5] (1859-1952) believed in utilizing flexible steps of problem solving. These steps are not absolutes, but tentative in their application. The teacher is a guide and stimulator to implement the following flexible sequence in problem solving:

1. Identify and clarify a relevant problem.
2. Gather data or information to solve the identified problem.
3. Develop a hypothesis. The hypothesis is tentative and not absolute.
4. Test the hypothesis to determine its completeness and accuracy.
5. Revise the hypothesis if necessary, based on evidence.

Integration of subject matter instrumental to the solving of problems is highly salient in John Dewey's philosophy of education.

E.L. Thorndike[6] (1874-1949) emphasized selected laws of learning, applicable in the science curriculum. Through experimentation and research, Thorndike developed and emphasized four laws. The law of recency stated that, all things being equal, the bonds are strengthened between the stimulus and the response (S–>R) the more recently subject matter has been learned. The law of frequency emphasized bonds being strengthened between the stimulus and the response, if the same subject matter had been learned again and again. All factors would have to be constant and the only variable being the very recent learning of subject matter, as compared to that which had been learned earlier. As a third law, the law of readiness stated that the bonds between the stimulus and the response would be strengthened, all things being equal, if the learner can benefit from the new subject matter to be taught. Opposite of benefiting from the new subject matter taught would pertain to the content being too complex. The bonds between the stimulus and the response can then not be strengthened. The law of effect emphasized that the bonds are strengthened in S—>R if the learner is satisfied and content with what has been learned.

S–>R theory of learning tends to fragment knowledge in terms of precise, measurable objectives for students to attain. The measurement movement has been very strong in education since the days of Thorndike's productive experiments. The slogan becomes, "Only what can be measured should be learned."

Early advocates of placing science in the curriculum included Jean Jacque Rousseau, a French philosopher.[7] Rousseau, (1712-1778) believed science to be the core of the curriculum. In his day, the classics with a rote learning emphasis was predominate. Rousseau frowned upon customs and traditions in eighteenth century France. In Rousseau's book *Emile*, the author advocates a single tutor per child. The child is to learn from the natural environment. Questions are raised by the pupil pertaining to what is of personal interest. The teacher is not to lecture to the student, but assist the child to find answers to his problems. Science equipment needed is made by the child with the tutor's assistance. Pupil freedom was an essential part of Rousseau's philosophy.

A second advocate of the importance of science in the curriculum was Thomas Henry Huxley.[8] Huxley (1825-1895) was greatly influenced by Charles Darwin's findings in the letters book *The Origins of Species*, published in 1859. Huxley believed that his native country England had its prosperity and hope built upon the ideas and principle of science. He believed that only what can be verified should be taught. It is immoral to teach to others what cannot be verified. Subjective content then is not to be emphasized in the curriculum.

A third early advocate of science being the core of the curriculum was Herbert Spencer (1820-1903).[9] Spencer, in England, was also greatly influenced by the research of Charles Darwin in his book *The Origin of Species*.

Spencer applied Darwin's concept of the survival of the fittest to human beings in society. Governmental aid should not be given to individuals in society, according to Spencer. Rather, through evaluation, the best and brightest would survive problems and difficulties in life. The human race would then improve itself, as weak members would be weeded out. Social Darwinism was a concept coined to attach meaning to Herbert Spencer's philosophy.

Spencer emphasized that students should receive as little lecture and as few explanations in classes as possible. Rather, each student should find out for himself/herself the answers to questions and problems. Learning by discovery and inductive teaching would be teaching strategies that Spencer would adopt.

Herbert Spencer emphasized five goals for individuals to attain in his essay, "What knowledge is of most worth?" First of all, each person should learn to preserve the self. Maintaining good health and survival in life then become highly salient objectives. Secondly, each person should learn to earn a living and the necessities of life, such as food, clothing, and shelter. Thirdly, each individual should become capable of rearing and disciplining children in the family. Fourthly, learning to live in society and abiding by laws in society are important. Fifthly, each person should learn how to utilize leisure time wisely. With these five goals of Spencer, science as a curriculum area becomes of utmost importance. For example, in goal number one which is preserving the self, certainly the area of science in general, and medical science more specifically can be highly significant.

The Modern Science Curriculum

There are numerous questions which need to be asked pertaining to the science curriculum.

1. How much of the separate subjects, correlated, fused, and/or integrated experiences should be emphasized?
2. Which philosophy of education, from the separate subjects to the integrated curriculum would best meet each student's learning style?
3. How can quality sequence be emphasized in ongoing lessons and units?
4. What can be done to secure student interest in learning?
5. Which means of appraising student progress are recommended?
6. How can students perceive purpose in learning?

The balance of this chapter will emphasize content in the integrated science curriculum. With integration, specific philosophies advocate relating subject matter more so than others. With integration of content from the learner's own unique perception, a psychological science curriculum is emphasized. Learners themselves are involved in achieving sequence or order in the curriculum. With student input into ongoing lessons and units, interest develops to provide effort in learning. Evaluation needs to consider the total student with his/her academic, social, emotional, and physical development. This includes appraising purpose or reasons learners develop for achieving.

The integrated science curriculum is a way of thinking about teaching and learning. It represents a definite moving away from stressing the separate academic discipline of biology, chemistry, physics, astronomy, botany, zoology, ecology and geology, among others.

The science teacher needs to be a stimulator to motivate students to identify problems and questions. These problems and questions relate to an ongoing lesson or unit of study. The stimulus may be the utilization of an audio visual material or a science experiment. If students, for example, are studying a unit on "The Changing Surface of the Earth", a related film strip may be shown. When the filmstrip, after proper introduction by the teacher, is shown to students, the latter are encouraged to identify problems and questions. A major goal in showing the filmstrip is to stimulate higher levels of cognition. Students may then select problems such as:

1. What causes volcanic eruptions to occur?
2. How do the lava, ashes, smoke, and cinders affect plant and animal life?
3. Why are different kinds of rocks formed as a result of these eruptions?
4. How is the natural environment altered from volcanic activity?

After vital problem areas have been identified, the science teacher needs to assist students to gather needed information to secure answers. A wide variety of materials needs to be utilized. These include reading materials (textbooks, library books, pamphlets, as well as science and regular encyclopedias), and audio-visual aids (laser video discs, video tapes, slides, films, models, objects, and excursions). Materials used need to be of interest to and on the understanding level of pupils. Each student must learn from materials which are meaningful and understandable. Their science teacher becomes a guide and assists students to obtain information related to the problem.

Students may volunteer to serve on committees of their own choosing to solve identified problems. For each of the four problems listed above as examples, volunteers may work on a committee to obtain subject matter necessary for problem solving. Additional problems will arise as problem solving opportunities are ongoing.

After adequate content has been obtained, students should be guided by the science teacher to develop a hypothesis. The hypothesis represents a tentative answer on conclusion to the stated problem. A careful statement of the hypothesis is necessary. The hypothesis covers the data or information gathered. Haphazard and effortless hypotheses must be avoided. Hasty conclusions do not represent the methods of science.

Each hypothesis is to be tested through experimentations, demonstrations, reading, and/or the utilization of audio-visual aids. Hypotheses may be modified, refuted or accepted, as objective evidence warrants.

Problem solving methods of teaching science emphasize:

1. identification of problems regardless of which academic disciplines are involved;

2. obtaining of information from a variety of reputable data sources to solve the identified problem. Critical and creative thinking are involved when securing data directly related to the problems. Appraisal of information is a must;
3. developing a hypothesis, tentative in nature, based on the information obtained. The hypothesis represents one or more generalizations reflecting fairly and objectively the data gathered for the establishment of the hypothesis;
4. testing the hypothesis and truly noticing in an unbiased manner what has transpired;
5. modifying the hypothesis if evidence warrants. Evidence is a key concept when the hypothesis is tested in terms of its consequences.

Problem solving is a vital philosophy to emphasize in a quality science curriculum. A second philosophy, namely, the use of behaviourally stated objectives in teaching and learning science, has selected merits. These include:

1. The objectives or ends of instruction are precise and stated in observable, measurable results. After instruction, the science teacher can measure if a student has or has not attained a specific end.
2. The selection of learning opportunities which must harmonize with the objectives. Otherwise, the learning opportunities are not valid for students to attain the objectives.

Selected limitations to the use of precise objectives in teaching science include the following:

1. They are limited in what can be stated in measurable terms. Too frequently, factual knowledge becomes the heart of the behaviourally stated objective movement.
2. They are weak in emphasizing processes, such as creative and critical thinking, as well as problem solving. Processes occur within the individual and observable measurable results may accrue in the statement of the problem, the gathering of data, developing of a hypothesis, the testing of a hypothesis, and revising of the hypothesis. However, the flexible steps of problem solving in many cases do not

allow themselves to be stated in terms of precise objectives. Problem solving as a process is internal and not subject to measurement.

An idea centred science curriculum could also be emphasized. With an idea centred science curriculum, subject matter objectives receive major emphasis. Development of the mind or intellect becomes of primary importance. Cognitive ends, rather than affective or psychomotor, are stressed in ongoing lessons and units. To achieve cognitive ends, rather heavy use of reputable science textbooks, workbooks, and additional reading materials become paramount. Other materials, such as the use of experiments, demonstrations, models, objects, excursions, and audio-visual aids (slides, filmstrips, films, and video-tapes, among others) are utilized as needed to aid students to achieve well intellectually.

Diverse levels of intellectual growth may be emphasized in ongoing science lessons and units, such as students acquiring facts, concepts, generalizations, and main ideas.

With an idea centred curriculum, it is necessary to emphasize the following:

1. Abstract learnings acquired by students need to be applied in concrete situations. The concrete situations may well stress the heart of the science curriculum-students being involved in testing hypotheses within the framework of science experiments.
2. Relevant subject matter. Trivia needs to be weeded out. Generalizations that are vital need to be supported by significant facts.

Decision-making as a fourth philosophy needs to be stressed in ongoing science lessons and units. Thus, each student needs to have ample opportunities to choose which objectives and tasks to pursue in an open ended science curriculum. The student is also heavily involved in appraising the self in teaching-learning situations. The science teacher must have as a major objective to develop within the student the desire and skill to make choices and decisions. Lecture and the heavy use of explanations are opposite of assisting students to make decisions in terms of what to learn as well as means of learning. What the student selects as objectives, learning opportunities, and evaluation procedures may emphasize the solving of problems, the attaining of measurably stated objectives, and/or the acquisition of subject matter. Values clarification of issues in science is of prime importance in a science curriculum emphasizing making choices and decision-making.

Decision-making by students in science can be further emphasized through the use of:

1. *Learning centres*. Here, students may sequentially select which sequential tasks to pursue and which to omit. Time on task is salient. A psychological, not logical, science curriculum is in evidence when students do their very own sequencing of learning opportunities.
2. Teacher-student planning of objectives, learning opportunities, and appraisal procedure in science. There needs to be very heavy input from students when these three parts of the science curriculum are planned.
3. *A contract system*. The teacher needs to assist, not dictate, to students in developing significant learning opportunities to pursue in the contract. The contract may be signed by both the student and the teacher with a due date for the project determined by the former.

For each of the above-named methods of emphasizing decision-making by students, relationship or integration of diverse academic discipline in science needs to be emphasized. The social sciences, humanities, and mathematics need to be brought into ongoing science lessons and units, when it is important and vital to do so.

In Closing

The attempt to correlate, fuse, and integrate subject matter has a long history. Science as a relevant curriculum area has a more recent history. Joseph Lancaster and the monitorial system of instruction in 1805 stressed relating certain curriculum areas such as reading, spelling and handwriting. Other academic disciplines, according to Joseph Lancaster, were taught as isolated from each other, such as subtraction from addition, as well as division from multiplication.

In the middle 1800's, the teaching of science initially was stressed as doing a better job of exercising the muscles of the mind (theory of mental discipline), as compared to the more traditional academic disciplines taught. Jean Jacque Rousseau, Thomas Henry Huxley, and Herbert Spencer were strong advocates of science being the focal point of instruction.

There are definite teaching strategies which reflect and emphasize the integrated science curriculum:

1. Problem solving strategies incorporate content regardless of the academic disciplines involved. Problems identified in science may well require subject matter from various subject matter areas in arriving at needed answers.
2. Precise objectives may be utilized in teaching to stress students acquiring vital facts, definitions, principles, and laws of science. Either learners attain or do not attain that which is stated within the specific objectives. Science teachers teach directly toward the specific ends of a lesson or unit. After instruction, the teacher measures if students have or have not been successful in goal attainment. Objectives need to incorporate the interdisciplinary science curriculum philosophy.
3. A subject centred science curriculum needs to emphasize relationships of ideas from diverse academic disciplines. From these abstract ideas, students may achieve well intellectually and develop relevant generalizations.
4. A decision-making curriculum in science is highly valuable for students. Life consists of making choices on an individual basis, from among diverse options and alternatives.

Notes

1. Shepherd, Gene D., and William B. Ragan. *Modern Elementary Curriculum*. Six edition, New York, Holt, Rinehart, and Winston, 1982, pages 82-84.
2. Ediger, Marlow , "The Lancastrian Monitorial System of Instruction", *Resources in Education*, ERIC Clearinghouse on Teacher Education, 1987.
3. Cubberly, Elwood P., *Public Education in the United States*. Cambridge, Massachesetts, Riverside Press, 1947, Pages, 388-396.
4. William B. Drake, *The American School in Transition*. Englewood Cliffs, New Jersey: Prentice-Hall, Inc., 1955, pages 347, 388 and 415.

5. John Dewey. *Democracy and Education*. New York: The Macmillan Company, 1961.
6. Gary A. Davis, *Educational Psychology*. New York: Random House, 1983, pp. 133 and 209.
7. John S. Brubacher, *A History of the Problems of Education*. 2nd edition, New York: McGraw Hill Book Company, 1966, pages 204-207, 215, 221, 260 and 354.
8. Christopher Lucas, *Our Western Educational Heritage*. New York: The Macmillan Company, 1972, page 436.
9. John T. Wahlquist, *The Philosophy of American Education*. New York: The Ronald Press Company, 1942, pages 36-37.

REFERENCES

Brubacher, John S. *A History of the Problems of Education*, 2nd edition. New York: McGraw Hill Book Company, 1966, pages: 204, 207, 215, 221, 260 and 354.

Cubberley, Elwood P. *Public Education in the United States*. Cambridge, Massachusetts: Riverside Press, 1947, pages: 388-396.

Davis, Gary A. *Educational Psychology*. New York: Random House, 1983, pages: 133 and 209.

Dewey, John. *Democracy and Education*. New York: The Macmillan Company, 1961.

Drake, William B. *The American School in Transition*. Englewood Cliffs, New Jersey: Prentice-Hall Inc., 1955, Pages 347-388, and 415.

Ediger, Marlow. "The Lancastrian Monitorial System of Instruction". *Resources in Education*, ERIC Clearinghouse on Teacher Education, 1987.

Lucas, Christopher. *Our Western Educational Heritage*. New York: The MacMillan Company, 1972, page: 436.

Shepherd, Gene D. and William B. Regan. *Modern Elementary Curriculum*, 6th edition. New York: Holt, Rinehart, Winston, 1982, pages: 82-84.

Wahequist, John T. *The Philosophy of American Education*. New York: The Ronald Press Company, 1942, pages: 36-37.

11

The Administrator as an Instructional Leader

School administrators have diverse responsibilities. A major responsibility should be to improve the curriculum. Students need to experience the best in objectives, learning activities, and appraisal procedures. Learners deserve the right to achieve optimally. Human beings have much worth and need to attain in an optimal manner in personal and social development. Each person needs to develop fully as an individual. Individuals need to achieve vital understandings (facts, concepts, and generalizations), skills (listening, speaking, reading, writing, and thinking), and attitudes (values, beliefs, and feelings). Persons also interact with others in society. Developing social skills then also becomes important. Each is a member of the societal arena.

Issues in Instructional Leadership

There are numerous issues involved in the concept of administration and curriculum development. One issue pertains to the extent of scope of administrators working in improving the teaching-learning situations. Thus, the school administrator could play a minor role as compared to a very extensive role in achieving an improved curriculum.

A second issue involving administrators .nd the school curriculum emphasizes which facets need to be diagnosed and remediated or changed. There are numerous curriculum areas. Within a specific curriculum area, there also are many points of intervention and modification. Careful consideration needs to be given in evaluating which area(s) of the curriculum need to be changed from what is to what should be. Quality leadership is needed in modifying the curriculum.

A third issue involves which philosophy or philosophies to emphasize in teaching-learning situations. Experimentalism stresses a problem solving philosophy. The school administrator, together with faculty members, need to identify curricular problems. Data must then be gathered in answer to the problem. A hypothesis or answer to the problem(s) should result. The hypothesis is tentative and subject to testing. After being tested the hypothesis is accepted, modified, or refuted.

Realism, as a philosophy of education, emphasizes the use of measurably stated objectives in teaching students. Results also advocate management by objectives (MBO) for administrators in achieving a quality curriculum.

Idealism advocates an idea centred curriculum. Textbooks, workbooks, and worksheets may provide major learnings for students to attain subject matter. Audio-visual aids, as learning opportunities, are good to the point that students achieve salient vital facts, concepts, and generalizations.

Existentialists advocate individuals learn to make personal choices and decisions. Whether it be students, faculty members, or school administrators, decision-making skills are needed, according to existentialists. Each person must accept responsibility for decisions made. A learning centre philosophy and/or teacher-student planning is then important in the curriculum.

Each of the four above-named philosophies differs much from the other. An issue then remains as to which school of thought administrators need to follow and which curricular decisions are to be made.

A fourth issue in school administration pertains to which psychology of learning should be emphasized in the curriculum. Behaviourism, as a psychology of learning, stresses the use of programmed learning. Small amounts of subject matter are learned before students respond to a test item. Feedback is given to students after each response made. Programmed learning can be emphasized in textbook form or software for computer use. Other forms of behaviourism include instructional management systems (IMS) and mastery learning. Each of these methods of teaching stresses the use of precise, measurably stated objectives.

Somewhat toward the other end of the continuum is humanism, as a psychology of learning. Humanists emphasize student input in selecting objectives, learning activities, and evaluation procedures. Teacher-student planning, as well as the utilization of learning centres, further stresses tenets of humanism. Students then need to learn the art of decision-making.

Additional psychologies of learning include Jean Plaget's developmental psychology and Jerome Bruner's recommendations of using inductive procedures in teaching students. An issue for school administrators then exists pertaining to which psychology or psychologies to emphasize in teaching-learning situations.

A fifth issue for school administrators pertains to how much emphasis should be placed upon staff development of teachers. A comprehensive, systematic approach may be utilized here. A definite scope and sequence involved in conducting in-service education programmes. Toward the other end of the spectrum, school administrators may place limited emphasis on staff development or delegate responsibilities in this area to other instructional leaders, such as a curriculum director or teacher mentors.

The Role of an Instructional Leader

School administrators as leaders in improving the curriculum must be able to work effectively with faculty members. A domineering leader cannot generally win the support of teachers and other workers in the school setting. Nor can an administrator be effective who avoids problems which need solving in the curriculum. These are two extremes which need to be avoided.

School administrators are models for others to emulate. This model emphasizes being highly knowledgeable about trends and issues in the curriculum. Enthusiasm for curriculum development is reflected within teachers. Enthusiastic principals and superintendents desire to discuss and reflect upon ideas in education with teachers.

The model of the school administrator also emphasizes definite attitudes of acceptance, respect, and tolerance. Teachers feel free to voice their opinions pertaining to recommendations, issues, and opinions in education. The administrator collaborates with teachers in developing the best of objectives, learning activities, and appraisal procedures. Trust between and among teachers and the principal or superintendent is definitely in evidence. Teachers feel they can come to the school administrator with their problems and anxieties to receive needed understanding and assistance.

The school administrator needs to be skillful in using techniques of in-service education to bring about positive changes in the curriculum. In-service education programmes too frequently are unsuccessful. Why? Teachers may perceive little or no purpose in their implementation. Topics pursued in these kinds of in-service programmes lack relevance for the classroom teacher. The dynamics and vitality of in-service education are lacking. Principals and superintendents rather need to work in the direction of in-service programmes which promote purpose and meaning. Teachers need to perceive in-service education as a means of becoming better instructors. Utilitarian motives must be perceived by the teachers in attending in-service education programmes. What is learned here can be applied in teaching-learning situations. The role of the instructional leader in in-service education is to assist teachers to perceive value in diverse kinds and programmes of in-service education.

Problems in Teaching-Learning Situations

To improve the curriculum, school administrators need to identify and solve problems pertaining to the classroom/school setting. Which problems then need identification and solutions?

Students achieve poorly in school due to a high absentee rate. Sequence is lacking then in understandings, skills, and attitudes acquired by the student. Teachers and administrators must work with parents to assist the latter to have their offspring attend school regularly. Parents need to be guided to see what happens to the student as a result of absenteeism. Undertakings, skills, and attitudes are sequential. Breaks in the sequence accrue with absences by the student. Students who are ill or cannot attend school need homebound instruction. Quality is a key word to emphasize in teaching students in the home setting by qualified teachers.

Tardiness also hinders student progress in school. Tardy students disrupt the classroom when they enter late. Vital tasks and experiences are omitted from the learner's experiences in situations such as these.

High rates of absenteeism and tardiness can make for future dropouts from school. When there is no apparent reason for a student being absent or tardy, problems, no doubt, will increase for these individuals. A potential dropout has little cause to be optimistic about the future.

A student who attends school may not perceive purpose in completing the high school years. Physically, but not emotionally and intellectually, the student is in school. Perhaps, these students are waiting for the day to drop out of school. School administrators need to be leaders to assist in developing a quality curriculum for those who cannot perceive value(s) in school attendance.

Other students who are at risk may achieve at an average and somewhat below average level of attainment, but feel it is important rather to earn money. Income from a job competes with the desire to achieve well in school. Ultimately, with heavy expenses, such as owning a car, the student decides to drop out of school and work full time. School attendance then competes with earning money. The latter ultimately has more purpose for the high school student. These students need identification, prior to dropping out of school. Objectives, learning activities, and appraisal procedures must be selected which aid the potential dropout to perceive schooling as being more important, as compared to earning money.

Pregnant teenage girls are becoming increasingly larger in number. Selected specialists state teenage pregnancy as being epidemic. Secondary school principals and superintendents need to take leadership roles in providing learning opportunities for these students. These activities assist in emphasizing the holding power of the school. The holding power, however, must emphasize a relevant curriculum, which assists pregnant teenagers to complete high school diploma requirements. Individual differences need to be provided for. All teenage pregnant girls need to attain as much as possible.

At risk students can include the gifted and talented. Too many of these students are not challenged in the school curriculum. The gifted and talented may then drop out of school. These situations are costly and expensive. A nation and a society lose out when the skills and abilities of the talented and gifted are not utilized. These individuals tend to take the lead in governmental positions, in industry, and in the professions. Each school system must identify the gifted and talented. A curriculum for the gifted and talented must be in evidence which assists to achieve optimally.

Students with drug abuse problems need appropriate guidance and counselling services. These students must be referred to specialized services when needed. Critical situations and moments are involved when students involved in drug abuse are left to cope for themselves. Lives, talents, skills, and persons are lost when students with drug abuse problems are left alone with little or no assistance given by teachers, administrators, counsellors, and the helping professions. Each person has worth and must be given assistance to achieve as well as possible.

Students who lack status or feel a lack of belonging within a group or class need attention. These students need assistance to work well with others. Carefully selected committees comprised of learners highly accepting of others can be a good starting point for an isolate or one who is on the verge of being an isolate. The student who lacks feelings of status should be asked to provide ideas or materials in which he/she excels. Most students have a skill that can be shared with others. Perhaps, a hobby or interest can be shared with others in the class setting. This is a way for the student to feel status and prestige. Perhaps, at the same time, this same student can develop feelings of belonging to a group or committee.

Certainly, school administrators need to assist teachers to guide each student to achieve well be they handicapped, average achievers, or talented and gifted. Human beings are a nation's most prized entities. Each needs to achieve as much as abilities permit to attain optimally in understandings, skills, and attitudinal goals.

In Summary

The school administrator, as an instructional leader, has vital, salient, relevant responsibilities. These responsibilities include:

1. resolving issues in leadership roles and responsibilities;
2. revealing appropriate roles to be an effective leader in instructional improvement;
3. emphasizing problem solving skills in curriculum development.

Principals and superintendents need to assist teachers to stress the following in teaching-learning situations:

1. Learning activities should be meaningful to students.
2. Learners need to perceive purpose in ongoing lessons and units.
3. Students should experience interest in the curriculum.
4. Individual differences among learners need adequate provision.

REFERENCES

Knezevich, Stephen J. *Administration of Public Education*. Fourth edition. New York: Harper & Raw, Publishers, 1984.

Krajewski, Robert J., *et al.*, *The Elementary Principalship*. New York: Holt, Rinehart and Winston, 1983.

Roe, William H., and Thelbert H. Brake. *The Principalship*. Second edition. New York: Macmillan Publishing Company, 1980.

Snyder, Karolyn J., and Robert H. Anderson. *Managing Productive Schools*. London: Academic Press, 1986.

Wood, Charles, *et al*. *The Secondary School Principal*. Boston: Allyn and Bacon, Inc., 1979.

12

Remedying Ills in Society

Society does expect public schools to remedy many of the ills in the societal arena. Criticisms are hurled frequently at public schools for evils which accrue on the state and national level.

The United States in five years time (1982-1987) has moved from the leading creditor to the leading debtor nation on the planet earth. The charge is made that public schools do not educate for the world of economics and economic competency. Comments, such as these, place unwarranted responsibility upon the public schools. Can any institution take responsibility for economic decisions made, other than governmental officials, in general? To be sure, public schools need to do the very best possible of educating each student to attain optimally. However, decisions made by officials in government may not be in the best economic interests of the nation. Deficit spending in which the deficits have more than doubled in seven years cannot be remedied by the public schools. All time high trade deficits are also in evidence during the years 1985-1987.

Educating for economic competency could become a major goal in education. All curriculum areas, in general, might then reflect the economic arena and a person's role in therein. The scope of the curriculum would then be narrow indeed. A broad, general education seemingly meets the needs of students individually more so than any other plan of curriculum organisation. It is difficult to move away from a scope and sequence which emphasizes the language arts, the social studies, science, mathematics, art, music, and physical education. With these curriculum areas, students achieve basic content which cuts across all academic disciplines. Thus, the language arts areas of listening, speaking, reading, and writing are salient in all curriculum areas in school, as well as being salient in society.

The concept of economic efficiency changes rapidly. What emphasizes the utilitarian and the practical stresses continual modification, revisions, and newness. Stability in the economic area is not in evidence. It is difficult for public schools to emphasize that which is vital and relevant in vocations, jobs, occupations, goods, services, trade, and interdependency in the economic arena, since change is so much in evidence.

Additional Problems in Society

A racial society is certainly in evidence. Minority groups receive less pay, experience more unemployment, and in general, the less of the good life, as compared to the dominant white race. Segregated or partially segregated areas in housing, education, and occupations are definitely in strong emphasis. Society has failed to integrate minority groups to experience the good, the true, and the beautiful. Since society has failed to develop the concept of equality among the races, the public school has had to assume this responsibility. Magnet schools and busing of students have been means utilized to integrate the races.

It would be much easier and utilitarian for society to work in the direction of *all* experiencing the good life, rather than public schools attempting to rectify that which is not justifiable, such as segregation of the races.

A second additional problem in the American societal arena is a rather high level of poverty. Poverty problems are relatively easy to observe in cities, large and small, as well as in rural areas. Poverty is due to many causes. Among others, these causes include racial discrimination in work opportunities, instability of jobs in society, as well as recessions and depressions. Paying a high per cent of one's expenditures on sales tax tends to work against the economically disadvantaged in society. The word *income tax* has become a highly negative concept in American society. The graduated income tax can be very fair and is based on the ability to pay. However, federal and state governmental officials believe the income tax to be sacred and should not be raised. The concept of *free enterprise* is also very sacred in society. Thus, the private sector is portrayed as being good while the public sector represents evil. Such reasoning is indeed erroneous. Federal and state governments must assume heavy responsibilities for the poor and the indigent. It is immoral to have street people, hungry and cold persons, as well as slum dwellings, and crime ridden areas. There is ample wealth to curb these ills. When people are taxed according to their incomes, amply money will be available to fund social security, take care of needs of the poor, have jobs for all who desire them, as well as provide medical, dental, and old age care for citizens in society. When the free enterprise system becomes an ideology and an absolute, its usefulness goes downhill. The free enterprise system (the private sector) and the pubic sector complement each other. They must not be at loggerheads. Governmental action is necessary when the free enterprise system divides people between the haves and have nots.

Students who come from poverty homes cannot do well in school. Approximately, twenty per cent of public school students come from economically disadvantaged homes. The public schools can do little to remedy the situation. Poverty level students can receive free noon meals five days a week from the school lunch programme. This is not adequate for a calendar year by any means. There are too many other times necessary for the intake of nutrition within a given year. Society fails in meeting the needs of poor people. Students in school must then have nutrition needs met, in part, through the school lunch programme. The public schools then attempt to remedy the ills of society. However, remediation is extremely difficult when students come from poverty areas. Student achievement in goals attainment goes downhill in different curriculum areas when society permits poverty in the home setting.

Child abuse seemingly is quite common. Each day in newspapers, cases of sexual, physical, emotional and social abuse are reported. Students coming from homes where abuse occurs cannot achieve well in school. Emotional scars of involved students hinder in goal attainment in school and in society. Teachers and principals are required by law to report suspected cases of child abuse. Those teachers and principals who report cases of child abuse may be received in a hostile manner by the parent(s). Parents know who the teacher is of the elementary school age pupil. The principal may not back the teacher in a confrontation with a hostile, angry parent. The teacher who reported the child abuse is left holding the bag.

Child abuse is a societal problem. Students will have a difficult time to grow up as productive adults when in the school years, child abuse occurs in the home setting. The public schools are required to accept the role of reporting suspected cases of child abuse. Wrongs and ills in society place additional responsibilities upon school personnel. Counselling of students has long been a tradition in the public schools.

Sexually transmitted diseases are indeed a great problem in society, especially AIDS. AIDS is deadly in that a person's immune system does not function. Without an effective immune system, a person with AIDS has little hope of surviving, except for a short period of time.

Public schools have taken additional responsibilities in implementing instruction pertaining to AIDS in the curriculum. Objectives, learning activities, and evaluation procedures must be selected, planned, and implemented in ongoing lessons and units of study.

Both parents work in securing income for a family. The two paycheck family is a necessity in many cases. Sometimes, job/professional opportunities emphasize both parents be in the world of work. In single parent homes, the bread winner also is not at home when children arrive from school. The latch key child then may not see the parent(s) until later on in the evening. These children must be by themselves from the time the school day ends until the parent(s) arrive at home. Sometimes, parents leave for work before the child leaves for school in the morning. The child does not get the security, attention, and the educational opportunities that the home should provide. The public schools are asked to make up for deficits of experiences for latch key children. Thus, a public school has a programme of games and educational activities for pupils, starting at the end of the regular school day until later on in the afternoon, when parents arrive home from work.

There appears to be much criticism of the public schools and their endeavours. And yet, the public school is asked to take on increased responsibilities. The latch key programme represents an increased responsibility for the public schools. Society has failed to provide for children where both parents work. The public sector in terms of governmental assistance and money tries to get out of many programmes of aid to domestic spending. It is continually reinforced in the news media that the private sector can do things better, more efficiently, and economically. The private sector, however, has been unwilling to take over responsibilities in child care. Generally, the private sector wants lower taxes, cheaper costs of labour, benefits for industries locating in a given area, and increased profits. Child care cannot be measured on a profit basis. To be sure waste and inefficiency are not advocated. But, if children are to achieve well in school and develop into productive citizens, an adequate investment will be needed for child care. Thus, needed provisions must be made for latch key children. Latch key children fending for themselves can be dangerous and harmful. Rather, a quality programme of educational opportunities for latch key children needs to be in the offing.

Numerous public school systems offer courses in parenting on the secondary school level. General and specific objectives, learning activities to achieve the objectives, and evaluation procedures to determine student programmes have been developed in lessons or units on parenting. With hild abuse, latch key children, and home poverty, more and more educators recommend parenting skills be taught in school. Too many children come to the school setting with meager educational background experiences. Nutrition needs also have not been met in the home setting. Being a good parent is important in any society. Children of today become the parents of tomorrow. The societal arena too frequently has failed in parents rearing offspring properly and appropriately. Thus, the public schools are called upon to assist students to learn about what makes for good parents. The public schools here operate in a manner to correct ills in the societal arena.

Early intervention programmes exist in selected states. Early intervention programmes operate in terms of assisting parents to work effectively with their offspring, ages birth to three years. Resource people, with appropriate educational background and training, visit parents in the home setting. Hopefully, parents will, as a result of the resource assistance, be better able to offer stimulating educational experiences to the infant. Early intervention programmes are based on the beliefs that infants can do better in public school achievement when content learned is sequential from birth on. Thus, education of the young does not start on the kindergarten level, but at birth. Parents need guidance to provide sequence in the experiences of the young child from the crucial time of birth to the beginning of the public school years. After the public school years begin, parents have tremendous responsibilities in helping their children achieve optimally. The public schools are heavily involved in remedying neglect of education of young children in the home setting.

Television has certainly failed to educate children in the home setting. The television industry could do much to help educate public school students in their homes. The TV media instead focuses upon violence, sex, drug abuse, alcoholic beverages, and robbery, among other ills. If models are important for student to learn from, television has its negative input. Parents in the home setting also fail to set an example by watching television programmes with their children that have an unhealthy impact.

The public schools must come to the aid to rectify unwholesome ideas that students receive from TV. TV basically has had little to teach students in terms of vital subject matter, mortality, and quality social development. Thus, the public school curriculum needs to stress appropriate intellectual, social, emotional, and physical growth of students.

Programmes viewed on television reflect the demands and interests of the lay public in society. If the consumer desired more wholesome TV programmes, content therein would change to the positive. It is doubtful if the present listing of TV programmes would survive if parents and others in society demanded presentations of positive educational value. Television with its rapidity of quick adventure, movement, and interest hinder students from completing or doing well in homework. Basically, what is on television is transitory, insignificant, and possesses entertainment qualities largely.

The schools need to develop a curriculum which is quite opposite of programmes on television. Thus, the public school curriculum should emphasize:

1. Conflict resolution through peaceful means.
2. Respect for others regardless of race, creed, or religion.
3. Goodness, beauty, and truth in its manifold dimensions.

The above-named three standards apply also to attempts in alleviating societal trends of wars and rumours of wars, as well as problems in human relations among individuals.

Further societal problems which the public schools need to attempt to rectify include:

1. Juvenile delinquency, teenage pregnancy, and suicide.
2. Ageism and sexism.
3. Counselling of troubled and maladjusted students.

In Closing

The societal arena brings on many problems which need solutions. Much is demanded of the public schools in working toward solutions. The public schools have become scapegoats for what society cannot accomplish and do. It becomes absurd to blame the public schools for huge governmental budget deficits or for unfavourable imbalance of trade with other nations. No doubt, society will increase their demands upon public schools due to increased ills in society. Society needs to be wary of expecting too much from schools, especially with the very limited amount of funding available for doing the job. The following are unrealistic demands:

1. Teachers solely being accountable for students achievement. There are many other individuals (parents), agencies and institutions which must accept thorough responsibility for a student's achievement in school. Poverty, hunger, abuse, and parental unemployment are highly negative factors in assisting students to do well in school.
2. Schools being completely responsible for drug abuse and consumption of alcoholic beverages by students. Adults in society present a rather negative role model in substance abuse for young people.

13

Parent-Teacher Conferences and the Pupil

There is a very important way by which parents can maintain close contact with the teacher of their children in the school setting and that is through parent-teacher conferences. Parent-teacher conferences should be held throughout the school year as the need arises. These conferences may occur in the following ways and times:

1. when the school sponsors parent-teacher conferences generally toward the beginning of a new school year;
2. when the school schedules a particular evening for open-house involving patrons in the district to attend;
3. when the parent and/or teacher feel a need to talk together concerning a child's progress in school. This conference can be held in the school setting or the use of the telephone may save time for involved individuals.

Thus, concerned parents must communicate with the teacher or teachers pertaining to problems that children face in learning. It is very frustrating and disappointing to parents and to the child if the latter does not like school and is not achieving well. Parent-teacher conferences may well be a way of remedying these situations.

The Setting for the Conference

It is of utmost importance that a relaxed environment be in evidence for these conferences. Generally, very little is achieved in outbursts of anger, in blaming others for past mistakes made, and in refraining from participating during a parent-teacher conference. Thus, it is important for parents and the teacher to respect the thinking of each other during this conference. The purpose of parent-teacher conferences then is to solve problems cooperatively relating to a child's progress in school. In an atmosphere of respect, parents need to describe as objectively as possible, the difficulties their child is experiencing in learning. Some of the common problem areas that may be discussed, depending upon their relevancy, include the following:

1. content learned in mathematics or reading is too difficult for the pupil. The learner is 'lost' in selected curriculum areas and needs to have learnings which are on his or her achievement level. Whatever is taught must represent new learnings for pupils; success, however, in developing new learnings is very important for each child;
2. a child may complain of being hit or pushed around rather continuously by another pupil;
3. the child may fear a stern, rigid teacher;
4. the child would prefer to stay at home rather than attend school.

Teachers are human beings. They teach many pupils in a school day. Professional teachers will want so speak with parents and provide the best educational experiences possible for children. Thus, good teachers will provide interesting learning activities in the class setting and help each pupil to achieve to the highest possible—intellectually, socially, emotionally, and physically.

Expanding the Use of Parent-Teacher Conferences

Results from any parent-teacher conference should help to improve experiences in the school setting for the involved pupil. Punishing pupils physically or reprimanding them orally to improve achievement is definitely not recommend. A child who is not doing well in school already feels enough punishment without adding to this burden. Pupils learn best if they are interested and see purpose in learning. Thus, results from parent-teacher conferences should result in happier children experiencing relevant, worthwhile learnings.

Too frequently, parent-teacher conferences have been conducted largely on the elementary level of schooling. It would be wise to extend these conferences through the secondary level of schooling. Approximately, thirty per cent of secondary students drop out of school before graduation. Of those who graduate, there, no doubt, are many students whose individual needs have not been met in the school setting. The secondary curriculum, too frequently, has not made provision for individual differences among students. Witness the following remarks that secondary teachers make about their classes:

1. a geometry teacher says his standards are high since 40 per cent of the students in his class fail the course. These are low standards indeed! All students should be taught so that as much geometry as possible can be learned successfully by each student. The teacher must teach rather than fail students. The teacher's role is that of teaching all students rather than attempting to sort learners into passing and failing categories;
2. a history teacher states that students in his class must be able to read and comprehend the textbook(s) he has selected for the course. This teacher states that being able to read content well is the only way of learning history; if students get below 80 per cent of the test items right on tests given by this teacher, 'D' or 'F' grades will be the end result on report cards. For many learners in this class, the selected textbook(s) generally will be either too difficult to comprehend or lack challenge for the more talented learners. There are other ways of learning history other than reading from selected textbooks. Thus, films, filmstrips, tapes, pictures, transparencies and the overhead projector, and discussions are additional ways of learning. The cut-off point as to who should get A, B, C, D and F grades is arbitrary.

There are many reasons why students get low grades. The following, among others, are some of the reasons:

1. the content was too difficult for students to learn;
2. the class was not taught in a manner of providing for differences in intelligence and capacity;

3. the test(s) were poorly written and did not cover what had been taught;

4. test items were too difficult for students to reveal what had been learned.

Thus, parent-teacher conferences may be just as beneficial on the secondary level as compared to the elementary level of schooling. Again, the overall purpose of having these conferences is to provide satisfying relevant learnings for each student.

14

Administrators and the School Secretary

School administrators have numerous responsibilities indeed in improving the curriculum. Quality objectives, learning opportunities, and appraisal procedures need to be in the offing to guide each student to achieve more optimally. Administrators then need to be able to work effectively with all teachers to improve the curriculum. Principals and superintendents are leaders in the school setting. Secretaries in the school also are vital people in meeting challenges to support a quality environment for administrators, teachers, support personnel, and other workers in the educational arena. Each secretary needs to contribute to provide an environment from which each professional and other workers can do their best to make the school a stimulating, meaningful place to educate all students to achieve in an optimal manner.

The School Secretary and a Quality Environment

Each secretary helps or hinders others in the school setting from doing their best. To be sure, there needs to be fair treatment of secretaries. Each secretary must be respected and appreciated for accomplishments made. Now, it is up to the secretary to possess attitudes which assist in developing an atmosphere in which positive feelings exist. Too frequently, the school secretary is:

1. rude to all personnel except the school administrator. She believes that her job is dependent upon one variable only

and that is to please the principal of superintendent. A much higher level of morality involves perceiving of and respecting the many variables or persons in the school setting. Each person, be it teachers, support personnel, or other worker, desires and wants to be respected;

2. indifferent to needs of teachers in the school setting. If the school secretary is the only person named to mimeograph or photocopy necessary materials for teaching, he/she might be highly indifferent toward these needs. In other words, the secretary refuses to do the required work for all, but the school administrator. The quality of instruction goes downhill due to the attitudes of the school secretary;
3. hostile to people in general. Teachers and other workers in the school setting are intimidated and desire to have as little interaction with the school secretary as possible. The hostility of the secretary develops an environment of mistrust.

The school administrator may not know this situation exists or he/she might refuse to change the hostile attitudes of the secretary. Perhaps, the school administrator feels it is good to have perfect cleavage between the school secretary versus the faculty and staff. It might even be that the school administrator feels safer in his/her position when concerns of workers in the school are directed against the secretary and not the administration.

What needs to be done to improve the quality of a school secretary's services? The authors have selected recommendations.

1. School administrators need to realize that secretarial behaviour affects teachers, support personnel, and other workers in the school setting. How a secretary relates to the administration in a school is important. Effective relations need to exist here so that quality endeavours to improve the curriculum can be the lot of principals and superintendents. However, a rude secretary's behaviour to others in the school setting makes for a negative environment. Stress, tension, and anxiety may well be an end result for teachers and other school workers.

Administrators need to have conferences with each school secretary to develop quality standards of behaviour for the latter.

Periodically, the principal or superintendent must evaluate with the secretary if the criteria are being met. Feedback from line and staff is important here in evaluating the effectiveness of a secretary's work.

2. The administrator needs to appraise if the school secretary is fulfilling needed obligations to teachers. Each teacher must have his/her request filled pertaining to needed mimeographed or photocopied materials used in teaching-learning situations. An unwilling secretary should meet required obligations for seeing to each teacher receiving needed materials for teaching and learning. Demands upon any secretary must be realistic. An adequate number of responsible secretaries need to be in evidence in any school setting. It is a definite *must* that the secretarial staff assist teachers to do the best job of teaching possible.
3. If a school secretary is hostile toward people in general, a complex situation exists. The social administrator needs to have a series of conferences with the secretary to implement criteria to improve attitudes. If the attitudes of the secretary do not change quickly, he/she must receive notice of terminating the employment. The school secretary has tasks to complete relevant to the position. Secretarial positions are important to facilitate the goals of the school. A major goal is not to provide a job per se to any person. Rather, each secretary needs to realize his/her position is highly important in developing a quality curriculum. Honest public relations programmes assist in implementing relevancy and vitality in the educational enterprise.

Responsibility and the School Secretary

To whom is the school secretary responsible? Generally, it has been believed that the secretarial staff is solely responsible to the school administrator only. The writer would like to challenge these beliefs. If the secretary is responsible to a principal or superintendent only, a brutish individual could be charming and pleasant to the administration alone, and offensive toward others. Would situations such as these aid in developing a quality environment among employees within a building? Hardly. The authors believe it is quite apparent that the role(s) of the school secretary affect many in the school setting.

There are definite recommendations to make in responsibilities secretaries have toward others in achieving quality in a school environment.

1. each secretary needs assistance to perceive how his/her deeds and acts affect others in the school setting. The ripple effect should be clearly explained to the involved secretary. Adequate time needs to be spent with the school secretary to guide the latter to understand that deeds and acts do not cause vacuums. Rather, there is cause and effect to most human behaviour;
2. the secretarial staff must realize that positive human relations are important. The secretary that exhibits negative nonverbal as well as verbal behaviour may well set the tone for sequential behaviour within others. The authors were well acquainted with a secretary's nonverbal behaviour which was highly offensive to teachers. A quiet groan was made by the secretary for work she did not want to engage in. Incidentally these offensive groans together with sharp unfriendly piercing eyes made all teachers avoid coming to the office, even for highly necessary communications. The only exceptions here in coming to the office were that teachers very quickly checked their mailboxes and left;
3. administrators should assign selected secretaries to give assistance to teachers. A secretary might then be accountable to three or four teachers. Too frequently, the senior secretary wants to become an administrator and force other secretaries to do all the secretarial work. This wastes the work that needs to be done, secretarial in nature, by the senior secretary playing the role of administrator or supervisor rather than performing significant secretarial work.

Competent School Secretaries

Each secretary needs to be hired on the basis of possessing definite competencies. Too frequently, secretaries are hired on the basis of being a prestigious friend or relative to someone. A secretary may also be hired on the basis of being a girl friend or confidant. However, these are wrong criteria in employing secretaries in the school setting.

1. Secretaries should be of good character within the cultural setting. Each secretary can be a model for others to emulate. Being friendly, moral, helpful, and competent are traits that are admirable in any secretarial position in school.
2. Each secretary, prior to employment, should demonstrate necessary skills to be a productive member of the educational enterprise. Too frequently in typing, secretaries
   - *(a)* reverse letters. There are so many corrections to be made by a proof reader that it is impossible to cull out all the errors. Each secretary needs to type and proof his/her work carefully before presenting the final copy to the administrator or a set of teachers. Slovenly prepared work by a secretary merely pushes the work of proofing on others. Secretaries need to be quality proofreaders whether a typewriter or word processor is being utilized;
   - *(b)* leave messy products which are unimpressing to say the least;
   - *(c)* skip lines in typing... A rush attitudes is involved here. Secretaries need to give of their best in typing;
   - *(d)* do not listen when instructions are given to revise a test. The needed revisions are then not made;
   - *(e)* make up rules of their own in terms of roles and responsibilities. The writer believes profitably employed people in a polite atmosphere need to be in evidence. Secretaries must not be principals, superintendents, or business managers. Rather, the school secretary has a vital role in facilitating the school and the curriculum toward optimal accomplishment.

In Summary

Secretaries are human beings. They need respect, encouragement, and rewards. Each secretary must be remunerated adequately for quality services performed.

The authors have attempted to diagnose specific areas of concern in the work of school secretaries. These areas include rudeness, indifferences, and hostility as attitudes aimed toward others. Secretaries have definite responsibilities in the school setting. They are responsible to school administrators, teachers, support personnel, and other workers in the educational enterprise. Competent secretaries who are desirous to work should be hired for the school to function adequately.

Definite standards need to be developed cooperatively by teachers and the school administrator which must be followed by the secretarial staff. If a secretary cannot fulfil the criteria, he/she may well need to be replaced.

15

Philosophy of Kindergarten Education

Kindergarten is a very valuable part of a student's education. Here, the student has left the home setting for a definite period of the day to be with other learners of a similar chronological age. The young child also interacts with a qualified teacher, certified to teach on the kindergarten level. An aide may assist the kindergarten teacher in teaching pupils. Diverse philosophies of kindergarten education are in evidence in present day schools.

History of Kindergarten

Friedrich Wilhelm Froebel (1782-1852) has been called the originator of kindergarten education. Froebel emphasized a definite philosophy of instruction. He believed that young learners should be active participants in learning. Too frequently in Froebel's day, students were passive in listening to teachers' lecture. Physical punishment was utilized to discipline students. Students suffered from blows received from teachers. Rote learning and memorization were methods used to teach students.

Friedrich Wilhelm Froebel emphasized respecting and liking children. Children should enjoy learning. Games needed to be utilized to assist pupils to like school. Rather than pupils being evil beings, Froebel advocated that children were born as good individuals. Freedom was very important for pupils in the kindergarten. Froebel was fond of nature. At one time, he was apprenticed as a forester. Kindergarten, meaning a garden for children, is very close to the idea and concept of nature.

Froebel had definite materials made for use in teaching. These materials assisted pupils to achieve the major goal of becoming creative individuals. The first kind of materials were called *gifts*. The items here pertained to the world of mathematics. One kind of gift was six spheres. To Froebel, the sphere represented perfection. There are no edges on a sphere. A point in the centre is equidistant to all points on the surface of the sphere. Pupils were to be creative in using the spheres. A second kind of material called gifts was a set of cylinders. Each cylinder had smaller cylinders inside. The smaller cylinders could be pulled out and put back together again to make the large cylinder. A third kind of material called gifts emphasized the use of cubes by pupils. Each cube could be separated into smaller cubes and put back together again to form the large cube. Additional gifts were physical representations of lines, points, and planes.

The teacher, according to Froebel, was not to dictate to pupils uses for the gifts. Rather, pupils were busy utilizing these materials based on their own creative needs and purposes. However, pupils were required to place the small cylinders inside the large one, or the small cubes were to be put back together to make a large cube, after each separate learning activity. The form or shape of gifts could not be changed.

A second kind of item emphasized in Froebel's kindergarten was called *occupations*. Several occupations were engaged in by pupils. Materials comprising occupations changed in form or shape when utilized by kindergarten pupils. One kind of occupation emphasized pupils putting different colours of dots to make a pattern on paper. Or, pupils would string beads of different colours and shapes. Paper could be folded and different designs cut with the use of scissors. As an occupation, Froebel was very strong in recommending clay modelling by pupils. All of these activities stressed the use of materials in which the form or shape changed physically.

As a third kind of activity for kindergarten pupils, Froebel advocated the use of mother play songs. When pupils sang a song, such as content on gardening, they would creatively dramatize the tilling of the soil, planting of seeds, watering the plants, and hoeing the weeds. Sometimes, pupils would hold hands and form a circle when singing songs. Froebel was struck by the idea of having pupils in a circle. The circle, like the sphere, represented perfection in geometrical figures.

Friedrich Wilhelm Froebel believed that schooling should represent joyous occasions for learners. Play and learning needed to be integrated. Kindergartners should be spontaneous, creative, and free.

Opposite of Froebel's thinking would be:

1. physical punishment of pupils;
2. rote learning of subject matter;
3. a teacher determined curriculum;
4. a formal school environment.

The kindergarten was to be a place where pupils enjoyed ongoing learning opportunities. From within, pupils had much say so in how the gifts and occupations were to be utilized. Pupils were to feel safe, secure, and loved. On Froebel's tombstone are the words "Come, let us live for our children."

The Open Curriculum in Kindergarten Education

Kindergarten education can emphasize a very informal curriculum in today's schools. The teacher then becomes a guide or stimulator. His/her job is to motivate, encourage, challenge, and secure pupil interest in learning. The informal classroom structure may emphasize the use of learning stations in the classroom. Each station is quite open ended in terms of what pupils may achieve.

A variety of kinds of materials abound at each station. Concrete (objects and items), semi-concrete (audio-visual materials), and abstract materials (library books) are located at each station. Pupils have considerable freedom in decision-making as to which tasks to pursue sequentially. The learner's own interests and purposes aid in deciding which learning opportunities to pursue. The following are examples of the kinds of stations contained in a classroom:

1. *A library book centre*: Here, pupils may listen to a story being read by the teacher in a stimulating manner.

Illustrations are shown to learners in the book as the contents are read orally by the teacher or an aide. Selected objects on the table relate to content in the library books. Thus, a few model animals at this station relate directly to the content being read from the library books. The models are also discussed with pupils.

2. *A drawing centre*: Diverse art media are at this centre. The media include pencils, crayons, magic marker, coloured pencils, and watercolours. Creatively, the learner chooses what to portray as an art product on paper. Spontaneity and uniqueness of expression are desired in terms of processes emphasized in art work. Pupils may wish to tell of content in the finished art product. Sharing of ideas with other learners is to be encouraged.

3. *A model centre*: Models of animals, buildings, and people should be housed here. Learners may take the models to build diverse scenes. The models may also be discussed in terms of characteristics and traits. Pupils may secure additional ideas about each model by consulting picture books with large illustrations. Ideas secured should be shared with other learners. Oral communication needs to be encouraged at each station.

4. *Role playing centre*: Toy dishes, plates, utensils, a kitchen sink, and refrigerator, among other items may well provide stimulating materials for pupils. Spontaneity of learners needs to be encouraged as they prepare and serve food to each other in a simulated setting. Quality of positive interactions is important in role playing activities.

Additional stations for the kindergarten pupils include:

(a) a reference materials station containing illustrated content for pupils;

(b) a costume station. Here, kindergartners may dress up in different costumes, such as in adult dresses, suits, slacks, shoes and hats;

(c) a construction station where pupils may enjoy making diverse objects. The materials utilized need to bear the understanding level of pupils. Necessary skills are possessed or can be developed by learners to construct and to make.

An open ended curriculum tends to emphasize existentialism, as a philosophy. Existentialists believe that:

1. each person needs to decide upon appropriate courses of action;
2. decisions and choices are to be made by the learner. The teacher is a stimulator and guide to assist pupils to learn.

A Subject Centred Curriculum

Selected kindergarten educators recommend a subject centred curriculum. A skills centred curriculum is then in evidence. In the area of reading, kindergarten pupils, when ready, would achieve the following skills in word recognition:

1. *Phonetic analysis*: Her pupils would learn phoneme-grapheme relationships. Phonics skills would be selected by teachers for kindergartners to learn to associate sounds with symbols.
2. *Syllabication*: To identify new words, pupils divide words into syllables. Unknown words may become familiar with the identification of each syllable within a word.
3. *Picture clues*: A pupil that does not recognize a word may identify the unknown with the use of pictures contained in a basal reader.
4. *Configuration clues*: A basic sight vocabulary of words are developed by the learner. Mastering these words cuts down on reading errors made by pupils.
5. *Context clues*: Kindergartners need to learn that a word pronounced must make sense with other words in sequential sentences.

Comprehension skills need to be emphasized as readiness of kindergarten pupils permits. These include reading to:

1. acquire facts;
2. secure sequential ideas;
3. obtain directions;
4. develop generalizations;
5. make predictions;
6. think critically.

A subject centred curriculum emphasizes pupils attaining abstract rather than concrete ideas. Pupils of kindergarten age with quality readiness experiences may achieve skills necessary in learning to read. A formal programme of reading instruction is then in evidence. A definite scope and sequence has been identified and is implemented. Scope and sequence in kindergarten becomes an inherent part of later grade levels in sequence.

A subject centred curriculum tends to minimize.

1. concrete and semi-concrete learning opportunities;
2. a hands on approach to learning;
3. the real world of experience;

Subject matter learned in mathematics could emphasize

1. the operations of addition, and possible subtraction, for kindergarten pupils;
2. the commutative property of addition;
3. drill and practice pertaining to subject matter learned;
4. problem solving on the understanding level of pupils.

Textbooks, workbooks, and photocopied exercises could provide major learnings for pupils in the mathematics curriculum, when emphasizing a subject centred curriculum.

Social studies and science units should have a predetermined scope and sequence for pupils. Definite subject matter objectives need to be in the offing for pupil attainment. Learning activities for kindergartners should assist pupils to achieve objectives. Evaluation procedures emphasize the degree to which pupils have achieved the subject centred goals. Cognitive objectives are predominate in a subject centred curriculum. Affective and psychomotor goals receive little or no attention in teaching-learning situations.

Measurement Driven Instruction

Measurement driven instruction (MDI) has received considerable attention in the educational literature. MDI emphasizes the use of precise, measurable objectives for pupil attainment. These specific ends have been predetermined for learners to attain. On the district level, instructional management systems (IMS) with its measurable stated objectives have been written for pupil achievement. Generally, the objectives have been identified several months to a year before their implementation in the classroom. State mandated objectives may also stress precise objectives for learner attainment.

Behaviourists with their emphasis upon MDI believe that whatever is taught to students can be measured. Through instruction, a pupil has or has not achieved an objective. It is then verifiable if an objective has been attained.

MDI has received emphasis on the kindergarten level of instruction. The emphasis upon instruction is toward the ends in MDI, not the learning activities, par se. Learning activities are important only as they guide pupils toward goal attainment. What pupils are to learn is stated in the measurable objective. Evaluation is done strictly in terms of the measurably stated objective. Advocates of MDI align the learning activity with the objective. Validity and reliability are two concepts strongly emphasized when appraising pupil achievement in terms of objectives.

Educators who disagree with MDI believe the latter to:

1. emphasize excessively predetermined objectives for pupils to attain;
2. stress excessively that pupil achievement be measured. Internal interests, purposes, and goals of learners then are not important;
3. eliminate pupil involvement in selecting objectives, learning activities, and appraisal procedures;
4. minimize the spontaneity and interests possessed by students;
5. emphasize a teacher determined curriculum.

In Closing

Three distinct philosophies of kindergarten education were:

First of all, an activity centred curriculum was stressed. Here, pupils are actively involved in selecting goals, learning opportunities, and appraisal procedures. A variety of materials to learn from and readily apparent in a stimulating learning environment.

A second philosophy stressed the importance of pupils learning subject matter. Definite subject matter is prescribed for pupils to attain. The scope and sequence of the kindergarten curriculum has been prescribed for the young learner. Subject matter to be learned is strongly emphasized in the predetermined scope and sequence.

A third philosophy emphasizes measurement driven instruction. Precise objectives are developed first in the kindergarten curriculum. The teacher then selects and aligns learning activities which guide kindergarten pupils to attain the objectives. Evaluation is emphasized only in terms of the measurably stated objective(s). Ideally, the stimuli in the learning activity should not exceed what is continued in the measurably stated objective. Emphasis is placed upon *measuring* observable outcomes of instruction.

Friedrich Wilhelm Froebel (1782-1852), labelled as the father of the kindergarten movement, advocated creativity as the major objective of education. Certainly, formalism was in evidence in Froebel's educational thinking. He stressed, for example, that a larger cube taken apart had to be put back together into a large cube, before learners could move on to a new learning opportunity. However, for his day in particular, Froebel was highly creative in stressing originality of experiences for pupils in using gifts, occupations, and mother play songs.

To synthesize diverse philosophies and beliefs in the kindergarten curriculum, the authors recommend that pupils have:

1. ample opportunities to choose interesting, sequential learning opportunities;
2. stimulating experiences which develop intrinsic motivation for learning;
3. opportunities to learn to read and write when readiness is in evidence;
4. sequential experiences which are meaningful in the arithmetic curriculum;
5. experiences broad in scope and appropriate in sequence pertaining to science, social studies, physical education, art, and music. A narrow curriculum of the so-called basics or essentials is not adequate in modern society.

16

Issues in Microcomputer Use in the Classroom

Selected issues need addressing pertaining to the utilization of microcomputers in the classroom setting. Software technology is becoming increasingly common in the schools. Individual school buildings as a unit, as well as the city or country school system must address problems involving the increased use of microcomputers.

Student-Microcomputer Ratio

How many students should there be for each terminal in the classroom? For example, if lessons in mathematics are taught, what is an effective number of microcomputers which need to be available? The authors in supervising student teachers have asked cooperating teachers, as well as other teachers and administrators a recommendable ratio of students for each microcomputer. The answer varies from two to four pupils for each microcomputer. Presently, in the United States a 78 to 1 ratio is generally reported. Complex scheduling is in evidence then to guide students in learning from diverse programmes in software. Certainly, an increased number of microcomputers are then needed so that more pupils may benefit from this mode of instruction. However, as the number of microcomputers increases, additional problems become apparent.

1. Are classrooms adequate in size to house needed microcomputers? In a 5 student to 1 ratio, five microcomputers need to be in evidence for a set of twenty-five students.
2. Are an adequate number of repair/service personnel available to take care of malfunctioning of computer technology?
3. Will teachers truly utilize microcomputer instruction when an adequate number is available in the classroom? There may well be learning activities emphasizing traditional methodology which are as effective as microcomputer technology. For example, in drill and practice activities in arithmetic, flash cards as well as workbook and textbook utilization might be as proficient as software and microcomputer instruction. The latter, however, could also be used to emphasize varied experiences for students in the drill and practice arena.
4. Can software truly fit in to a specific lesson in terms of sequence or order? Or, does the teacher need to tailor make each learning activity in terms of where an individual learner is presently in actual achievement?
5. How does a logical curriculum in which a programmer has developed sequential steps for students to achieve in software content harmonize with the involved learner's style of learning? Do selected pupils achieve more effectively with a psychological curriculum? In a psychological curriculum, the involved student is involved in decision-making as to which activity comes first, second, third, and so on in ongoing lessons and units. To harmonize then with the student's personal style of learning, a variety of activities need to be in the offing from which a student may select to participate in a psychological curriculum.

The Teacher and Microcomputers in the Classroom

The role of the instructor has changed with the rather rapid increase of microcomputers in the instructional area. Another material has then been added for pupils' interaction and experience.

The teacher needs to be skillful in grouping students to use microcomputers effectively in the classroom. With a range of seventy to twenty students for each personal computer in a school, the instructor must manage or organise effectively for teaching and learning. Each learner needs guidance to achieve sequentially in programmed instruction.

Secondly, software needs to be catalogued in a manner whereby each programme can be secured readily. The chosen programme needs to fit in to the student's present needs whether it be drill and practice, diagnostic and remediation, games, simulations, or tutorial. The appropriate software for a student must harmonize with his/her present level of progress. A programme that is exceptionally easy or complex will not provide sequential learnings for the involved student.

Thirdly, the classroom teacher needs to have necessary knowledge and skills to operate a microcomputer. Unnecessary delays in placing software into the microcomputer or not knowing what to do when minor problems occur can provide situations in which pupils become restless and inattentive. Time on task for learners is salient. Distracted students may have a difficult time attending to microcomputer instruction if needless problems occur when changing from one learning activity to the next. For example in changing from a reading experience involving textbook use to the utilization of the microcomputer, the delay between the two activities must be sequential and not hinder instruction. Instructional materials need to be ready and available to optimize student learning.

Fourthly, relevant standards of conduct need to be in evidence in the classroom. Students need to learn to respect each other not only as an instructional goal but also in that it assists each learner to achieve as much as possible. Thus, students working sequentially at a terminal must desire to help each other learn in an orderly manner. Cooperation between and among students is important when pursuing microcomputer instruction.

Fifthly, the teacher needs to notice and record achievement from each student after a programme has been completed. Increased, sequential achievement is desired from each student. The school and classroom setting must have an instructional atmosphere in which each learner may achieve and progress. Post-achievement results can be compared with present progress when making comparisons of a student's achievement in programmed learning.

Dennis and Kansky[1] wrote:

> The computer can assume major responsibility for the control and direction of an individualized teaching environment. This application of the computer in the role of teacher is called computer-managed instruction (CMI) and covers a myriad of teaching duties. The mechanics of CMI include diagnosis of a student's learning level or of specific gaps in the student's understanding of a given topic. This diagnosis is linked to a prescription which could be placement in a certain study group or assignment of a learning task to be executed with suitable materials and teacher input. If instruction requires the use of limited resources (laboratory stations, machines, etc.), the computer can schedule those resources in a manner which not only optimizes their use but also ensures regular maintenance or repair. CMI can be used to route students through an entire curriculum, the routing of any individual student being adjusted to the student's achievement, interests, and learning style by means of regular evaluation. As individualization within large groups makes increasing demands upon student-teacher and student-student communication, the computer can facilitate that communication by providing "electronic mailboxes" for all participants. The computer can keep track of the academic progress or perils of individuals and groups in ways which the teacher may quickly and regularly use as a basis for modifying instruction, overriding computer decisions, changing the materials of instruction, and working with individuals as individuals. The record-keeping features of CMI also can be used to generate written reports for the student, teacher, parents, or school system.

Sixthly, it is excellent if a learner can receive a printout from programmes completed. These printouts, of course, are not available from numerous programmes. Hopefully, a printer will be an inherent part of a microcomputer so that the involved student may reflect upon printout results as a learning activity. Reviewing what has been learned previously is significant and a printout of programme results may well provide each student an opportunity for review.

Seventhly, how much time should students spend on microcomputer learning in each major academic area? There are educators who believe that a major portion of each day for a student may be spent on a terminal pursuing sequential programmes. Toward the other end of the continuum, numerous teachers and supervisors believe that microcomputer use be utilized along with other equally important activities, such as textbooks, library books, workbooks, and audio-visual aids, excursions, resource personnel, and worksheet use. Certainly, an adequate number of microcomputers and sequential software for each curriculum area needs to be in evidence prior to advocating a major portion of the day being devoted to microcomputer instruction. Social development of students in interacting with other human beings is salient. Committee endeavours for students then need to be stressed. There are many media from which pupils may learn; microcomputer methodology is one means for students to attain objectives.

Improving Software Quality in the Curriculum

There are definite improvements that need to be made when emphasizing a quality microcomputer curriculum.

1. In a frame emphasizing students finding the area of a circle, the circles should fit the geometrical description and not be ellipses. Also, the diameter or radius of the circle on the screen should be given. It may be highly complex for students to measure accurately the needed radius or diameter on the monitor. Accuracy of geometrical figures is very important in software development.
2. User friendly as a concept needs stressing in software development. Thus, if subject matter is presented on the screen pertaining to a famous president, prime minister, or king, students in a response should definitely not need to type the name of the leader on the keyboard in answer to a question about the content previously read. The computer will not accept the response unless the name is typed in with no errors in spelling. It would be highly recommendable to rather have a multiple choice format in which the involved student types in a, b, c, or d depending upon which is the correct answer to a question covering the subject matter read by the pupil on a previous sequential frame.

3. To advance to the next sequential programmed item, a student should not need to press the return key as well as the space bar. Rather, pressing either the return key or the space bar should be adequate to pursue sequentially in the programme.
4. Outline maps, worksheets, and workbook pages for students to complete, after the software presentation has been covered, should be a part of student learning. Thus, follow up activities, in sequence, should aid in clarifying and reviewing of content presented in software form on the monitor of the microcomputer. It is also recommendable that manuals for software be comprehensive in terms of background information and objectives for learner attainment.
5. Students should have the option of deciding if they want sound (a buzzer sound if a correct response has been made) or not when working on a programme. To provide for individual differences, a pupil may or may not wish reinforcement with a specific sound made. Microcomputer use should not disturb students who are working on other tasks in the classroom.
6. Learners should be able to control the speed of sequential learning within a programme. Thus, a learner may at the beginning of a programme indicate with typing F (fast), A (average), or S (slow) in terms of desired speed in pursuing sequential items in the programme. Individually, a pupil may also pursue a programme at his/her optimal rate of speed.
7. A printout is desirable after a student has completed selected programmes. A peripheral for the microcomputer is then needed which is the printer. From the printout, a student may notice strengths and weaknesses in performance. Remedial work can then remedy the identified deficiencies.
8. Content appearing on the screen or monitor should be clear and unambiguous. Thus, a cursor should not look like a negative sign in arithmetic.

9. Adequate evidence needs to exist pertaining to writers having taken weaknesses out of a programme. Taking the bugs out is highly significant in software development. Misspelled words should definitely not appear on a screen. Carefully evaluated sequences within any specific programme is necessary.

Wright and Forcier[2] developed the following evaluation form to appraise software quality:

Courseware Evaluation Form #3

Programme name:——————
Indicate all that apply with yes or no:
Drill and Practice ——— Tutorial ———
Simulation ——— Tool ———

Interaction

1. Programme is personalized
2. User can stop at any time
3. User can see score at any time
4. User can select level of difficulty
5. User can review instructions
6. User can review past mistakes
7. User goes at own speed
8. Testing occurs periodically during programme
9. Programme can select level of difficulty through testing

Content

1. Appropriate subject matter
2. Appropriate for grade level suggested
3. No implied racial or sexual discrimination
4. Can reteach principles
5. Meets objectives (teaches what it is supposed to)
6. Applicable to more than one subject
7. Presents correct information
8. Programme is interesting
9. Programme is involving
10. Programme is realistic
11. Programme is educationally sound

Format

1. Clear documentation
2. Written instructions are short and concise
3. Lengthy instructions are subdivided
4. Programme uses reinforcement:

   Through sound

Through graphics

Through written text

5. Programme uses graphics appropriately
6. Programme format is consistent with objectives
7. Programme makes full use of computer's ability
8. User can run programme without help from teacher

Other

1. Programme can have more than one user at a time
2. Programme teaches first, entertains second
3. Programme is worth its cost

Teacher Developed Software

There are selected educators recommending teachers developing their own programmes. The classroom teacher is in the best position to know what students are ready for in terms of new learnings. Readiness for a new task must be in evidence for individual pupils to benefit from new content being presented on the screen.

The teacher should also be in the best position to know which learnings students can attain sequentially. If a new step in learning is too complex, the involved student may experience failure. Reinforcement in learning is then not in evidence. A problem that teachers do face, more so than a publishing company of software, is the time and money necessary to debug a programme. Thus, a professional programmer can use pilot studies in determining at which step or steps a programme is not sequential. In the pilot studies, students may reveal at which point the next step of learning was too complex. This is not to say that commercial companies do quality work in debugging a programme. The opportunities to do so, however, are more in existence as compared to a classroom teacher who teaches full time and writes one or more programmes on weekends or after school hours. Kemp and Dayton[3] wrote:

> Unlike human beings, computers are very particular about the accuracy of the instructions they perceive. A single misplaced letter or symbol can render a computer programme useless as an instructional tool. Therefore it is very important that CBI materials be thoroughly tested before they are released for broad use.

Errors such as these are called 'bugs' and the process by which they are located and removed is called debugging. This is best accomplished by letting a variety of people try the materials to see what types of problems might occur. Ideally these people should be representative of the leaners for whom the materials are designed and should go through the materials under the anticipated circumstances for their use. They should be asked to work through the programme several times, trying all of the options, so that each branch can be tested. In addition, they should judge the effectiveness of the instruction and the clarity of the documentation.

Programmes written by a teacher can definitely fit into an ongoing lesson on unit. The contents in the programme are then related to objectives emphasized in the curriculum. It will be more difficult to secure from a commercial company software that sequentially harmonizes with present teaching and learning objectives emphasized in the classroom. However, quality software is increasing in number in schools whereby choices of content can be made which definitely relates to what is presently being taught in the curriculum.

Time is an important consideration for any teacher. Teaching is a demanding profession. Much energy goes into quality instruction in any classroom. Energy may not be available to develop programmes by instructor. The "adding on" concept to a teacher's load might well distract from a teacher's ability and performance in teaching. Commercial companies hire programmers to write, edit, evaluate, and produce course software. Administrators and supervisors in schools need to emphasize the nomothetic (needs of the institution or schools and their goals), as well as the ideographic (personal needs of teachers) dimension. A balance needs to be emphasized between the objectives of the school and objectives of human beings.

In Conclusion

There are numerous issues involved in the utilization of microcomputers. Certainly, modern technology is here to stay and will continue to change. Hopefully, the changes will be for the good. Students individually need to achieve as much as possible in the curriculum. Microcomputer instruction may well be a means to guide students to achieve course goals more effectively. What will aid students to achieve and progress continuously?

1. each learner needs to be successful in learning by experiencing quality sequence in ongoing lessons and units;
2. reasons or purpose needs to be inherent in diverse learning activities;
3. challenging, interesting experiences need to be in the offing for pupils;
4. adequate provisions need to be made for slow, average, and fast achievers in an atmosphere of respect;
5. students must understand and attach meaning to what is being learned;
6. learners need to experience balance in the curriculum. Thus, understandings, skills, and attitudinal goals need to be stressed adequately in the curriculum.

Lockard, Abrahams, and Many[4] wrote:

> With appropriate and effective courseware, the computer can become an integral part of the learning process. It can assume a portion of the teaching responsibility, becoming a student's private tutor. In turn, this may free the teacher to spend more time with individual students. However, to achieve such a goal assumes the availability of excellent courseware.

After identifying courseware of potential interest, a review or evaluation process is critical prior to purchase. The ideal approach is to begin with advice or recommendations from experienced users of a given product. Next, other reviews of the package may be helpful. Finally, a hands-on evaluation is required, unless it is absolutely impossible to obtain the materials.

Notes

1. J. Richard Dennis and Robert J. Kansky, *Instructional Computing*. Glenview, Illinois: Scott, Foresman and Company, 1984, page 13.
2. Edward B. Wright and Richard E. Forcier, *The Computer: A Tool for the Teacher*. Belmont, California: Wadsworth Publishing Company, 1985, page 160.
3. Jerrold E. Kemp and Deane K. Dayton, *Planning and Producing Instructional Media*. Fifth ed. New York: Harper and Row, Publishers, 1985, page 255.

4. James Lockard, Peter D. Abrahams, and Wesley A. Many, *Microcomputers for Education*. Boston: Little, Brown and Company, 1987.

REFERENCES

Dennis, J. Richard and Kansky, Robert J. *Instructional Computing*. Glenview, Illinois: Scott, Foreman and Company, 1984.

Kemp, Jerrold E. and Dayton, Deane K. *Planning and Producing Instructional Media*. Fifth edition. New York: Harper and Row, Publishers, 1985.

Lockard, James, Abrahams, Peter D. and Many, Wesley A. *Microcomputers for Educators*. Boston: Little, Brown and Company, 1987.

Wright, Edward B. and Forcier, Richard E. *The Computer: A Tool for the Teacher*. Belmont, California: Wadsworth Publishing Company, 1985.

17

The Counsellor in the School Curriculum

The school counsellor is a truly valuable professional to assist students to achieve optimally. Students experience personal problems which hinder achievement in the academic and vocational curriculum. Students may also encounter social problems. The social problems in its many dimensions can certainly make for a lack of progress in the school curriculum. The school setting represents a social setting with many involved human beings. If social relations are inadequate for a learner's satisfaction, goal attainment in the curriculum may well falter. The balance of this chapter will stress problems faced by students in the school setting. The role of the counsellor will be emphasized in these problematic situations.

Problems Experienced by Students

Teachers and administrators need to be careful observers of student behaviour. Students with complex problems need to be referred to the school counsellor. An open door invitation given by the counsellor must be available to all students. Students need to feel comfortable and welcome when meeting with the counsellor. The student and the counsellor realize that conferences held are strictly confidential. An atmosphere of openess exists between the counsellor and the counselee. Feelings of freedom are in evidence for the student to reveal thoughts, feelings, and values. The counsellor has feelings of empathy and understanding toward each counselee. He/she is highly accepting of others. Biases and prejudices toward people are not traits which good counsellors possess. A quality counsellor is able to accept students of diverse creeds, religious beliefs, and socio-economic levels. He/she is able to work effectively with students, as well as school administrators, teachers, and other school workers in solving problems of learners in the school setting.

One type of problem faced by students is loneliness. These students tend to be isolates or on the fringe areas of having any friends. Students who shy away from others in the school setting or those who try but cannot make friends need assistance by the guidance counsellor. In a relaxed environment, the isolated student and the counsellor need to identify the problem(s) involved. Cooperatively, ideas should be presented in attempting to solve the problem of loneliness. Bibliography library books may also be suggested for the student's personal reading. A plan of implementation needs to be developed to assist the student to develop feelings of belonging. Creative traits of the student must not be sacrificed in developing friendships with other students. Students who are very open-minded in relating socially to others might be assisted to seek out and accept the lonely student. Follow-up conferences with the isolate is important to determine progress made in guiding the student to develop feeling of belonging.

A second type of problem faced by students is a lack of esteem. Others seemingly do not notice or reward talents possessed by a student. These students may have numerous talents and abilities to offer. Or, that which is within the learner has never been brought to the surface. The learner possessing talents which are not rewarded by others may lack charisma or polish. He/she just cannot bring others to the point and place of recognizing inherent talents which are valuable, worthwhile, or utilitarian. Other students may reward a learner's talent(s) that are not as accentuated or positive. Life in its many dimensions is not often rational nor equitable. Students who have not been able to reveal their talents or abilities need assistance by the guidance counsellor to develop appropriate strategies. Reinforcement theory may be helpful here. The teacher of the student with low esteem may offer a reward to the latter for showing specific talents and abilities. The guidance counsellor needs to work with classroom teachers to assist the latter in identifying creativity within students and have these talents come to the forefront.

All want to be recognized for progress and achievement. What lies within the learner and has not come to the surface must be recognized. Student's abilities need recognition. This is true if academic, social, emotional, and/or physical talents are identified and rewarded. Also, each student is unique and has uniqueness residing within. The unique interests of any student need praise and understanding.

A third type of problem experienced by selected students involves feelings of security. Students may experience the bully in school who attempts to be lord of all. The submissive student may feel insecure indeed. The bully may even use oppressive methods to attain his/her ends. The submissive student here may have no choice but to give in to the oppressor in selected situations. Freedom and the right to choose their own destiny should be the lot of all students. Generally, teachers are overburdened with too many students to teach and supervise to adequately notice the welfare of each. A few teachers and administrators may lack concern for the individual student. They are not conscientious in their concern for the right of each student or preoccupation with other goals has become paramount.

Programmes of in-service education on the rights and responsibilities of students in school are highly important. Students will tend to develop in a positive manner when they are respected and accepted by others in the school environment. Students have an obligation in return to work in the direction of having a mutually satisfying school environment. The oppressed student as well as one who does the oppressing needs guidance and assistance. Neither one is developing optimally by any means. The oppressed student may immediately respond well when the bully no longer has control over the former. In other cases, it may take a long time of assistance to develop positive attitudes within the student who has been heavily dominated by others. Being dominated may meet a personal need of the oppressed student. This presents a further problem for the counsellor and counselee to solve.

A fourth type of problem experienced by students is having physiological needs unmet. Proper nutrition is important for all students in order to do well intellectually, socially, emotionally, and physically. Hungry students cannot progress, achieve, and develop well. Students whose families are on or below the poverty level qualify for free or reduced prices of lunches. However, one nutritious meal, five days in a school week, may not be adequate. The counsellor may need to work in the direction of breakfast being served to students of low family income levels. Other students who choose to do so may then pay for eating school breakfasts. Poverty is an awful experience to endure. A lack of income in the home has many detrimental effects on students. The house lived in may not be fit for human habitation. A family may have to select between purchasing food or heating the home during the cold winter months. A lack of reading materials may also be in the offing in the home setting. No library books, newspapers, and news magazines may be the lot of the poverty level family. Clothes worn are of low quality and not suitable for ensuring temperature readings. The clothes worn may not be conducive to developing a good self concept on the part of the student. In general, living in poverty does not buy nor provide for good things in life.

The guidance counsellor will be limited in terms of what can be done to assist the home in securing an income level necessary to buy the good things in life. By good things, the authors refer to having a life style which helps an individual to achieve optimally. The guidance counsellor can aid students to meet selected physiological needs, such as sleep and rest. Those students who watch late television programmes or stay up late to visit with parents tend to feel sleepy and apathetic during class time. A student may even doze off in class unintentionally. In consulting with the involved student, the counsellor needs to help the former schedule his/her time in the evening. Time needs to be available to the student for recreation, meals, homework, and sleep in the home setting. In conferring with parents the counsellor should state the importance of each student having adequate sleep and rest in order to do well in the school curriculum.

A fifth type of student problem is drug abuse. Ruined lives occurs for those who utilize drugs which are mind altering. Intoxicating liquor consumption comes in the same category of being a mind altering substance. Crimes against property and people are a result of individuals involved in drug abuse. The abuser of drugs and the victims of drug abuse both suffer. Money is needed to support an expensive habit. Thievery and robbery are means of securing money to buy drugs. People are murdered and mugged by individuals under the influence of drugs. The perpetrator may not even be conscious of having committed these crimes. Automobile accidents occur frequently due to drivers being under the influence of drugs.

In addition to the high costs involved in supporting the drug habit, the physical body soon shows its effects of chemical abuse. The addicted person cannot quit on his or her own in drug abuse. To be rehabilitated is a painful process. The toll then is indeed great in consuming addictive drugs.

Teachers and counsellors soon observe traits of students who are utilizing mind altering drugs. These students lose interest in school. Achievement and progress in school go downhill rather rapidly. Students who abuse drugs lose out on friends, as well as fail to participate in social events.

Teachers and counsellors need to identify students, as soon as possible, who are utilizing mind altering drugs. Students need to be referred to drug rehabilitation centres. Human life and talents must not be lost to the tragedies of drug abuse. First of all teachers and counsellors need to identify those students who are in the drug abuse category. Clarity of identification is important. Cooperatively the counsellor, teacher(s), administrator, and parents must pool ideas on solving the drug abuse problem. The consequences of each approach needs thorough evaluation. A path of solution, from among alternatives, must be decided upon. The resulting hypothesis is tried out and tested. The student with the drug abuse problem needs to be the focal point in terms of rehabilitation and becoming a productive member of society with an adequate self concept.

The authors had identified students with specific kinds of problems which need counsellor assistance and guidance. These include the following:

1. lonely, isolated students in the school environment;
2. low self esteem;

3. lack of feelings of security;
4. inadequate meeting of physiological needs, such as food, clothing, and shelter;
5. drug abuse problems.

Numerous other problems of students which require identification and solutions include:

1. abused individuals in school and in society;
2. marital discord and/or divorce of parents and their affect on students;
3. poor study habits and a lack of interest in school work;
4. obesity of students;
5. discipline problems of involved students;
6. crisis situations involving suicidal tendencies and depression;
7. student lack of interest in the curriculum;
8. staff development which assists in truly providing for individual differences;
9. illness.

In Closing

To achieve more optimally, students must experience a positive environment in school as well as in the societal setting. The guidance counsellor has important roles to perform in assisting students to overcome problems, personal and social, so that adequate, continuous progress in school is possible. Teachers, administrators, and parents must be involved in identifying and solving problems of students. An increased number of responsibilities will be given to professionals in the school setting. However, unless problems of the student are minimized or solved, little progress in goal attainment of the school's objectives are possible.

18

Problem Solving and the School Administrator

Administrators in the school setting face diverse problematic situations. To most problems needing solutions, there are no right or wrong answers. Each problem is seemingly unique to the situation. Solutions to problems are not absolutes, but relative to the situation. Many persons desire simple solutions to complex problems. To be sure, selected minor problems are easy to solve. Others require depth data gathering to come up with needed solutions. Frequently, however, time is rather limited to come up with answers to complex problems.

Administrators need to be sensitive to identifying problems in the school environment. Problems exist and do need to be identified. Avoiding the identification of problems merely adds to troublesome situations in school. Courage to face and identify problems is significant for school administrators. To improve the curriculum of a school or school system, identification of problematic situations is important. Adequate data needs to be gathered to solve a problem. Sometimes, on the spur of the moment, solutions to problems need implementation, such as in a current discipline problem. Hypotheses (answers) to problems are tentative and subject to testing. Too frequently, hypotheses are perceived as being final and fixed. When hypotheses are tested, it is quite obvious that modification and change may be necessary. Thus, what works in one situation involving discipline may not work in a different case.

Administrators then need to be skilled in identifying and solving problems.

Discipline and the School Administrator

A major role of school administrators emphasizes disciplining students for misbehaviour. A student is sent to the administrator's office for disrupting other students in the classroom, for fighting on the playground, for using profanity, for stealing, and other infractions of rules. A teacher may be weak in gaining the respect of students and sends more students to the principal's office as compared to other teachers in the school setting. A particular student who has behaved appropriately previously may change in behaviour. The behaviour changes may be due to loss of friends, to sickness or death of a person in the home setting, to neglect and abuse from the parent(s), and to feelings of general insecurity. An endless number of reasons can be listed for misbehaviour in the classroom, including the physical and mental health of the misbehaving student.

A knowledgeable administrator attempts to look at causes for misbehaviour. The cause(s) may be detectable or be numerous, complex, or not identifiable. Causes must still be carefully considered. Social literacy training as one concept in school discipline emphasizes looking at causes from the point of view of the institution of the entire school or school system. Thus, there may be unnecessary and excessively strict rules. Rules and regulations in school need to be reasonable in number and in terms of quality standards. Existent rules should assist students to learn and to achieve. Sometimes, rules are there to show authority and power over students. The authors recommend strongly that principals and teachers look at the school and class setting to notice if standards of conduct being emphasized hinder student behaviour and achievement.

When causes reside within the school and classroom setting (extrinsic to the learner), a problem solving situation exists. A problem needs to be identified. Information must then be secured in answer to the clearly defined problematic situation. A hypothesis needs to be developed which is an answer to the problem. The hypothesis should be tested in action and revisions made if necessary. It is imperative for the school administrator and the teachers to utilize tenets of social literacy theory to minimize problems pertaining to discipline among students.

Problem solving is also necessary if situations of discipline reside within the student. How should infracture of reasonable rules and regulations by students be handled? A systemwide discipline policy takes time to study, analyze, develop and implement. If, after careful study, the school administration and teachers decide upon utilizing tenets of assertive discipline, reasonable criteria to follow need to be identified and communicated clearly to students. Students must understand and attach meaning to these standards. Administrators and teachers also need to agree in a flexible manner, how to handle the first, second, and third infractures of a standard or standards before the parent(s) are called to school to talk with the teacher and administrator about the student's misbehaviour. Agreement then needs to be reached by the parent(s) and teacher, as well as principal, on how to minimize discipline problems from the involved student.

Problem Solving and the Curriculum

A curriculum for students is not stable nor static. A changing curriculum will be in evidence. Why? Society changes in these modifications are reflected within the school curriculum. A rather recent innovation in society—the use of the computer—has made for changes in media utilized to assist student learning. Each classroom of students taught by a teacher is different, in degrees, from last years roomful of learners. Students individually change physically, socially, emotionally, and socially, as they progress through the sequential years of schooling. With the many changes occurring in school and in society, the curriculum must also change.

There are numerous curricular problems for administrators and teachers to identify and solve. These include:

1. emphasizing quality sequence in student learning;
2. stressing an integrated curriculum where desirable and feasible;
3. advocating scope (breadth of subject matter) which meets needs, interests, and purposes of students;

4. implementing balance among objectives, such as cognitive, affective, and psychomotor goals. Each of these objectives should be reflected within ongoing lessons and units;
5. favouring intensive, depth teaching rather than survey approaches in the classroom setting;
6. emphasizing a variety of evaluation techniques to appraise various facets of understandings, skills, and attitudinal learnings acquired by students. In solving problems pertaining to curriculum development, each student should be assisted to attain optimally.

School Attendance and the Principal

Excessive absences and tardiness can certainly hinder student progress. Teachers need to take more time to plan for what students have missed due to being absent or tardy. What has been planned by teachers needs to be implemented to take care of student deficiencies in sequential learning. The absent or tardy student should achieve new learnings rather than make up that which has been missed or omitted on a previous day or days of school.

What can be done to minimize unnecessary absences and tardiness? Certificates may be given on a weekly, monthly, or yearly basis for good attendance. Extrinsic motivational devices are utilized in these situations to encourage regular student attendance. To vary the reward approach to emphasize students attending school regularly, inexpensive badges and prizes may be given at selected intervals. The extrinsic reward is contingent upon regular student attendance in school. The school administrator may conduct faculty meetings or a workshop in guiding teachers to use rewards systems to encourage student attendance.

No doubt, the best approach in emphasizing good attendance by students is intrinsic motivation strategies. From within, students then have a desire to be in school and be there on time. Attitudes and feelings of learners reflect their desire to learn and to achieve. There are selected guidelines which may be utilized by teachers to develop student interest in learning. Thus, lessons and ongoing units should be exciting and challenging to students. Boring and routine learning activities need to be replaced. Each student experiences tasks which are interesting and fascinating. Drudgery is then not in evidence in curricular experiences for students. Students individually need to be successful learners. No one likes to experience failure. Rather with success in learning, sequence is experienced by students. New facts, concepts, and generalizations achieved are based upon and related to previously acquired learnings.

Too frequently, teachers emphasize the utilization of basal textbooks, workbooks, and worksheets as learning activities for students. Experiences in the classroom should also stress activity centred approaches in teaching and learning. The activity centred curriculum for students might well include dramatizing what has been learned, constructing models and dioramas of previously acquired learning, developing a mural or individual pencil sketches pertaining to content attained, as well as write diverse kinds of prose and poetry reflecting subject matter learned. An increased use of audio-visual aids (slides, films, filmstrips, and transparencies) may further increase interest in learning; the rate of absenteeism and tardiness may go down, hopefully.

The school administrator and the teacher have definite problems to identify and solve involving improved school attendance on the part of students.

Problem Solving and In-service Education

Administrators and teachers, as well as support personnel need to grow, learn, progress, and achieve. In-service education can spur individuals on the greater levels of progress. The principal needs to identify problems in the area of in-service education for school personnel. Teachers also need to be involved in identifying and solving vital, relevant problems.

A school administrator emphasizing a problem solving philosophy must show courage in stressing problem solving rather than the avoidance of identifying weaknesses and difficulties in the school and class setting. Democratic procedures need emphasis in that all who have a role in these problematic situations are involved in analyzing and acquiring solutions to perplexities and conflicts in the educational arena.

Which problems need identification and solutions through in-service education procedures? There might well be a need to emphasize peers helping other students achieve well in the classroom setting. An excessive number of students in any classroom makes it difficult to provide for individual differences among learners. Peer assistance in teaching individual students might well make it possible for the classroom teacher to spend more time with a specific set of students needing increased aid to achieve well in school. In-service education sessions can emphasize the implementation of using peers in teaching other students.

Adult, paid or unpaid aides, may also do well in assisting the regular teacher to help students achieve optimally in the classroom. If aides do not assist teachers effectively, what needs to be done then? A problem has then been identified and needs solution. The principal and the teacher(s) need to clarify the problematic situation. A discussion is held to shed light on the problem. The discussion may be considered as a data gathering technique in securing information directly related to the problem. A related hypothesis should result. The hypothesis might involve an in-service education programme for teacher aides in the classroom. After the in-service programme has been completed, the hypothesis may need revising. Workshop results might also indicate that aids are doing a better job of assisting teachers in the classroom as compared to previous times. If aides are doing no better than formerly as a result of the in-service education programme, they may need to be replaced. Aides are in the classroom to assist teachers to provide adequately for students of diverse interest and achievement levels.

The administrator needs to be a proficient solver of problems at the building level, as well as in the entire school system.

Problem Solving and Personal Needs of Teachers

Teachers have personal needs which can be quite difficult as compared to institutional needs of the school. An administrator generally would not be a trained, licensed counsellor. However, he/she can be sympathetic, have understanding, and show empathy to teacher needs. The human condition seemingly emphasizes that people have personal problems. The best of individuals experience major as well as minor problems.

The authors know an excellent combination room teacher for grades one and two. This teacher prepared well, worked effectively with young children, and got along well with other adults in the building. In August, three weeks before the new school year began, her husband left her. This teacher became distraught over the situation and resigned her position in this small rural city. Divorce seemingly can come to the best of individuals. Here was an excellent classroom teacher and divorce was shattering to her. Other people are not as overwhelmed with a divorce, but still experience trauma.

There are many other situations involving the human condition which truly hinder effective teaching. Numerous teachers have problems with aging parents. Selected teachers are very concerned about the welfare of parents who cannot take care of themselves properly. There is a drain of energy on the conscientious teacher's part in taking care of these parents. There can be a major decision which needs to be made in terms of home care versus care in a nursing home.

Death of a parent, child, husband or wife, can be another drain on the teacher's effectiveness in teaching. A sudden death from an automobile accident or heart attack takes its toll on human effectiveness. Lingering illnesses from cancer or strokes of a loved one certainly does affect how well a teacher teaches in the classroom. One of the authors was a fifth grader when his mother had a severely disabling stroke which left her paralyzed on the left-hand side and made speaking very difficult. She died twenty-two years later. That is a long time to suffer a complex disability.

Runaway children indeed affect the teacher in many ways. The authors are acquainted with a teacher whose daughter ran away from home. This teacher mentioned how difficult it is to accept the fact that a child ran away from home. The community may be rude to the parent in these kinds of situations which add to stress in life. Fortunately, the daughter returned home. But, what happens to a good teacher's style of teaching with a missing child?

Child abuse is a common topic in the news. If a teacher's child is abused, certainly, the administrator needs to be empathetic and understanding. He/she needs to listen, understand, and be sympathetic of the human condition with its uninvited trials and tribulations.

There are a few additional human conditions, the authors wishes to enumerate:

1. What should be done where an excellent teacher's health has deteriorated and thus affects the quality of teaching? Does a school dismiss teachers who come in this category?
2. Selected teachers who do a good job of teaching experience intervals of depression. Should these teachers look for a different position, other than teaching, since bouts with depression do affect teacher interaction with students?

The school administrator, as a problem solver, needs to realize the human condition. The human condition has its successes and failures. There are uninvited situations in life which affect the teacher negatively. These negative happenings definitely affect the quality of teaching in the classroom. The principal needs to develop and possess feelings of empathy toward teachers who experience the unfortunate at selected intervals in life. Being a good listener and desiring to help solve personal problems of teachers, the school administrator is indeed a highly valued person.

In Closing

The authors have attempted to enumerate definite instances in which the principal needs to have the knowledge, skills, and attitudes of wishing to solve problems. The goals of the institution (the school and school system) change rather continuously. Society has its rapid change rate. School cannot remain static but must incorporate desired, needed changes. Teachers and other school personnel also experience desired as well as undesired situations involving change. With change in school and in society, the school administrator needs to identify and hopefully solve relevant, vital problems.

REFERENCES

Cruickshank, Donald R. *Teaching is Tough*. Englewood Cliffs, New Jersey: Prentice-Hall, Inc., 1980.

Henson, Kenneth T. *Secondary Teaching Methods*. Lexington, Massachusetts: D.C. Heath and Company, 1981.

Joyce, Bruce, and Marsha Weil. *Models of Teaching*. Third Edition. Englewood Cliffs, New Jersey: Prentice-Hall, Inc., 1986.

Joyce, Bruce, *et al*. *The Structure of School Improvement*. New York: Longmans, 1983.

National Society for the Study of Education. *Staff Development*, Part II. Chicago, Illinois: The Society, 1983.

National Society for the Study of Education. *The Humanities in Precollegiate Education*, Part II. Chicago, Illinois: The Society, 1984.

National Society for the Study of Education. *Becoming Readers in a Complex Society*, Part I. Chicago, Illinois: The Society, 1984.

National Society for the Study of Education. *Education in School and Non-School Settings*, Part I. Chicago, Illinois: The Society, 1985.

National Society for the Study of Education. *The Ecology of School Renewal*, Part I. Chicago, Illinois: The Society, 1987.

National Society for the Study of Education. *Society as Education in an Age of Transition*, Part II. Chicago, Illinois: The Society, 1987.

19

Using the School Library

Students in the public schools need to learn to utilize resources in the library. Resources in a library may be utilized for personal enjoyment by the learner. The resources can also be used to solve personal and social problems. Bibliotherapy is a valuable concept in library usage. Through bibliotherapy students may gain greater insight into their own lives and accept limitations possessed. Library books and other materials in a library may assist students to free themselves momentarily from anxieties and tensions. Developing and maintaining quality mental health is highly important for all. Library resources may also provide information on career awareness and exploration. Vicarious learning may save students from experiencing the undesirable. Library resources can aid students to experience the real world vicariously, and minimize selected undesirable experiences. To achieve the above-named broadly stated goals, a quality library containing a variety of materials, printed and visual, need to be in evidence.

The Library and Individual Differences

Students differ from each other in many ways. These differences include capacity, interest, purpose, and achievement. Individual differences need adequate provision. Which reference sources should be in evidence in a quality library?

Library and trade books written on different levels of reading achievement are important. Students individually read at different levels of achievement. Thus, a library should house an ample supply of library/trade books possessing diverse levels of complexity. Each student must be able to locate a library/trade book on his/her reading level. Selecting a book on one's reading level indicates that meaningful comprehension of content is possible. Library/trade books must also emphasize a variety of topics. Students differ from each other in terms of interests possessed in pursuing an area of interest in selecting and reading sequential books in the library.

Methods of encouraging learner interest in reading need to be present. Bulletin board displays which appeal to students and stimulate good reading habits are a must in the library. Contents on these displays need to be changed frequently. An inward desire to read on the part of students should be an end result or objective of the bulletin boards. Librarians should be knowledgeable of student literature. They need to assist students to choose appropriate reading materials. Being able to suggest titles of books to students is vital. An enthusiastic librarian may certainly encourage learners to become greater consumers of literature. When students are pursuing problem areas or term papers, a helpful librarian can do much to assist students to locate significant related books.

For young pupils, a librarian should read books orally to these learners. A pleasant, enthusiastic voice in reading is important here. Illustrations in the book being read need to be shared with the young listeners. Eye-contact with these pupils as the oral reading progresses guides learners to feel important and wanted. Students of all ages wish to be accepted and have status. Ignoring requests for assistance from students presents a negative image for the librarian. Minimizing students' needs in utilizing the library emphasizes further weaknesses in services provided by an important institution in society.

The Library, an Instructional Materials Centre

A variety of kinds of materials for learning should be available in the library. Students have diverse learning styles. Concrete, semi-concrete, and abstract materials represent a classification system of the kinds of materials needed in a library.

With concrete materials, attractively displayed for all to see, students may learn from objects and models. These materials can be housed in display cases. An explanation of each object and model needs to be typed on a card. Librarians should be available to offer additional information as requested by students.

Semi-concrete materials should be abundant. Quality pictures, study prints, maps, globes, charts, software, slides, filmstrips, film, video-tapes, and video discs may provide needed subject matter for students. These semi-concrete materials need to be available to students as needed to secure necessary information. Librarians must be knowledgeable on audio-visual aids available to guide student usage of these materials. Appropriate places to use each audio-visual aid should also be in evidence. Comfortable furniture for student use to optimize learning must be an end result in utilizing the diverse materials housed in a library.

Abstract materials need to be abundant. Several sets of encyclopedias of recent copyright are a must. The encyclopedias are written for students. General encyclopedias, as well as special subject areas (such as science encyclopedias) need to be in the offing. Reputable daily newspapers and weekly news magazines should be conveniently accessible in quality libraries. Pamphlets, brochures, and other printed materials add to the quantity of abstract materials in a library. Librarians need to introduce students to assist them in finding needed materials.

Materials available in a library should meet the needs of students. Librarians must develop a personal philosophy of helping learners to achieve optimally. They need to guide students to locate and use materials in problem solving situations. A philosophy of service on the part of librarians emphasizes to be available as the need arises to assist students. Students need to feel welcome to come to the librarian to receive guidance and direction in finding and utilizing needed materials. A friendly, pleasant librarian within stimulating facilities for students should encourage learners to use concrete, semi-concrete, as well as abstract materials in ongoing lessons and units of study.

Criteria for Library Use

Libraries exist for the purpose of using their facilities to benefit individuals optimally. The materials are there for use by consumers to achieve a variety of purposes. Normal wear on materials in a library is to be expected. Libraries must be utilized effectively. The hours in which the library is open should benefit its patrons. A major goal of the library should be to encourage its use by students, faculty members, as well as administrators.

A quiet environment is necessary for those who are utilizing reading materials. The noise level needs to be such that students may comprehend ideas well. People who visit and disrupt the reading area hinder individuals from attaining worthwhile goals. Reading activities demand a quiet environment whereby the reader can accomplish diverse purposes in comprehending content. Librarians providing needed assistance to locate reading materials for students should do this in a manner which does not hinder the goals of those involved in reading

Objects and models on display should be placed in an area whereby students may discuss their observations with others. Students need to attain worthwhile learnings from these items. With discussions among students, higher levels of cognition may be an end result. Learners can gain valuable ideas from these interactions. Objects and models should be changed at intervals to encourage student observations and discussions. A library should be a fascinating place to be filled with materials of interest to learners.

Conference rooms need to be available. The conference rooms are for committee work involving students. Here, learners may compile their research on a problem area cooperatively. Story telling and the oral reading of library books to young students may occur in a conference room.

A librarian may meet with a group of learners in a conference room to explain the use of the library. After these explanations, the librarian can show students where the materials are located. This must be done in a manner which does not disturb those who are reading quietly in this designated area.

Classroom teachers will also wish to meet with students in a conference room in the library. For example, if a committee is doing research on a problem area, the teacher needs to consult with these students to determine progress. The conference needs to be held where the reference sources are located in the library. The teacher is then better able to assist students to find needed information close to where the materials are housed in the library.

Administrators and the school board need to support financially and emotionally the services and materials in the library. The library is a place to learn. It is a special area whereby students and school employees can go to secure printed materials and audio-visual aids. The library may aid individuals in getting materials to solve problems. It may also be a place to go to engage in sheer recreational reading. The goals and philosophy of any library should stress self actualization of the person. Each needs to realize his/her optimal level of achievement. Optimal progress may come in terms of understandings (gaining facts, concepts, and generalizations), skills (listening, speaking, reading, and writing), as well as attitudes (feelings, interests, values, and appreciations).

Negative philosophies involving use of the library are:

1. limited time in which students and school personnel can use its facilities;
2. meager number of materials available to consumers;
3. unfriendly, impolite services provided in library use;
4. cleanliness and neatness take the place of the actual utilization of concrete, semi-concrete, and abstract materials;
5. its unimportance in being properly funded.

The Use and Location of Reference Materials

Definite criteria need to be established in securing materials for a library. Too frequently, these materials have been obtained in a haphazard manner. A systematic procedure has not been utilized. A minimal use of the library may follow. Learners then lack enthusiasm in using many of the concrete, semi-concrete, and abstract materials housed in the library.

Criteria for obtaining materials in the library may well be the following:

1. the goals of instruction need to be achieved in diverse curriculum in the school;
2. a love for learning on the part of the students should be in the offing;
3. useful materials which are practical and have utilitarian values in the lives of students should be in the offing;

4. sheer enjoyment and appreciation of library materials is important;
5. a desire to develop and maintain a quality library represents the wants of learners;
6. input from students in terms of materials wanted for the library can make for intrinsic motivation on the part of students for library usage;
7. students need to assist in the operation of a well designed programme for library usage;
8. materials are purchased for use by students and not for storage alone, in the library;
9. methods to encourage consumer use of the library are important;
10. ease of checking out and returning materials is important in the operation of the library.

Numerous librarians and educators have started what is necessary to have in a quality library. Jarolimek[1] recommends the following reference source:

Books	**Miscellaneous materials**
1	2
Textbooks	Advertisements
Supplementary reading books	Magazines and periodicals
Picture books	Recipes
Biographies	City and telephone directories
Historical fiction	Labels
	Guidebooks and tour books
Special references	Letters and diaries
	Travel folders
Encyclopedias	Postcards
Maps and globes	Newspapers and news clippings
Atlases	Comic books
Dictionaries	Pictures
World Almanac	Schedules and timetables
Charts and graphs	Pamphlets and booklets (such

1	2
Yearbooks	as those from the information
Legislative manuals	services of foreign countries,
	superintendent of documents,
Junior Book of Authors	conservation departments,
Statesman's Yearbook	historical societies, art
Computers	galleries)
	Weather reports
Reference Aids	Manufacturers' guarantees and
	warranties
Card catalog	Money, checks, coupons for
The Reader's Guide	premiums, receipts
Bibliographies	Reviews, government documents
COMCATS	

Reference sources in a library should never remain stable nor static. Continuous evaluation of materials and services provided in a library needs to be in evidence. If a library does not increase its quality holdings, stagnation certainly will set in. Also, if services provided by a librarian do not change as new needs arise, a lack of improvement in its endeavours will hamper learner progress. Teachers, administrators, and librarians need to develop and maintain a library which will assist optimal achievement on the part of consumers.

Psychology of Library Services

The major schools of thought in psychology pertaining to library services provided, as well as use made of its materials, will be discussed.

Behaviourism, as a psychology of learning, is highly prevalent with state mandated objectives, as well as local instructional management systems (IMS). To assist students to attain precise objectives, the librarian can provide useful services in guiding learners to secure needed materials. These materials should assist students to attain objectives. The librarian must be familiar with and knowledgeable about the psychology of behaviourism. Thus, the librarian is in a good position to provide needed services to students. The reference sources provided by the librarian assist students to attain the stated, precise objectives.

As a second school of psychology in education, humanism has much to offer. Humanists, such as Carl Rogers, Donald Snygg, and A.H. Maslow advocate that students should be heavily involved in developing the curriculum. Several approaches may be utilized here. The teacher with his/her students may plan cooperatively what the latter are to learn in an ongoing unit of study. The emphasis is upon cooperation of students and the teacher planning objectives, learning activities, and appraisal procedures. A second procedure, using humanism as a psychology of learning, stresses a learning centres philosophy. An ample number of tasks at different learning centres needs to be available so that each learner may select what to complete and what to omit. Each student needs to be guided to be profitably occupied in sequential learning opportunities. A humane curriculum is in the offing if students have input in terms of which tasks to pursue and which to omit. A third method emphasized humanism could have the teacher list ten tasks (as an example) on the chalkboard. Students would be required to complete any four of the ten. This permits leeway for any learner to select what he/she deems desirable to complete and which to omit. A student could complete more than the four required tasks. Humanists advocate a wide variety of stimulating materials be utilized in an ongoing unit of study. Thus, at the different learning centres in a classroom, an abundance of concrete, semi-concrete, an abstract materials need to be in the offing. The librarian may certainly assist the teacher much in securing materials suitable for students at the different learning centres.

In Summary

A quality library is of utmost importance to learners in the curriculum. Definite criteria need to be met in library materials and services provided to consumers. The criteria include:

1. providing for individual differences among learners;
2. having a variety of concrete, semi-concrete, and abstract materials;
3. making the materials and services available to those who utilize the library;

4. providing for library use to individuals who possess diverse purposes and objectives;
5. emphasizing selected reputable psychologies of instruction in library usages, such as behaviourism and humanism.

Seating arrangements and furniture in a library need to be comfortable, useful, and purposeful. The major objective of libraries is to assist learners to achieve optimally emphasizing a variety of objectives.

Note

1. John Jarolimek. *Social Studies in Elementary Education*. Seventh Edition. New York: The Macmillan Company, 1986, pages 251-252.

REFERENCES

Glatthorn, Allan A. *Curriculum Leadership*. Glenview, Illinois: Scott, Foresman and Company, 1987.

Jarolimek, John. *Social Studies in Elementary Education*. Seventh Edition. New York: The Macmillan Company, 1986.

Lockhard, James, *et al*. *Microcomputers for Educators*. Boston: Little, Brown and Company, 1987.

Miller, John P., and Wayne Seller. *Curriculum*. New York: Longman, 1985.

Oliva, Peter F. *Supervision for Today's Schools*. New York: Longman, 1984.

Additional Reading

Bhaskara Rao, Digumarti (1994). *Scientific Aptitude*. New Delhi: Ashish Publishing House.

Bhaskara Rao, Digumarti (1995). *Animal Kingdom*. New Delhi: Discovery Publishing House.

Bhaskara Rao, Digumarti (1995). *Batracology*. New Delhi: Discovery Publishing House.

Bhaskara Rao, Digumarti (1996). *Scientific Attitude vis-à-vis Scientific Aptitude*. New Delhi: Discovery Publishing House.

Bhaskara Rao, Digumarti (1996). *Encyclopedia of Education for All*, 5 Volumes. New Delhi: APH Publishing Corporation.

Vol. I *Education for All: The World Conference.*

Vol. II *Education for All: The EPA-9 Summit.*

Vol. III *Education for All: Quality Education for All.*

Vol. IV *Education for All: Planning and Monitoring.*

Vol. V *Education for All: The Indian Scenario.*

Bhaskara Rao, Digumarti, Editor (1996). *Global Perceptions on Peace Education*, 3 Volumes. New Delhi: Discovery Publishing House.

Bhaskara Rao, Digumarti, Editor (1996). *National Policy on Education*, 2 Volumes, New Delhi: Anmol Publications Pvt. Ltd.

Bhaskara Rao, Digumarti, Editor (1997). *Care the Child*, 2 Volumes. New Delhi: Discovery Publishing House.

Bhaskara Rao, Digumarti, Editor (1997). *Education for the 21st Century*. New Delhi: Discovery Publishing House.

Bhaskara Rao, Digumarti, Editor (1997). *Reflections on Scientific Attitude*. New Delhi: Discovery Publishing House.

Bhaskara Rao, Digumarti, Editor (1997). *Scientific Attitude*. New Delhi: Discovery Publishing House.

Bhaskara Rao, Digumarti, Editor (1997). *Success Story of a Primary Education Project*. New Delhi: APH Publishing Corporation.

Bhaskara Rao, Digumarti, Editor (1997). *World Food Summit*, New Delhi: Discovery Publishing House.

Bhaskara Rao, Digumarti, Editor (1998). *Adolescence Education*. New Delhi: Discovery Publishing House.

Bhaskara Rao, Digumarti, Editor (1998). *Community and School Nutrition Education*. New Delhi: Discovery Publishing House.

Bhaskara Rao, Digumarti, Editor (1998). *District Primary Education Programme*. New Delhi: Discovery Publishing House.

Bhaskara Rao, Digumarti, Editor (1998). *Earth Summit*, 2 Volumes, New Delhi: Discovery Publishing House.

Bhaskara Rao, Digumarti, Editor (1998). *National Policy on Education: Towards an Enlightened and Humane Society*. New Delhi: Discovery Publishing House.

Bhaskara Rao, Digumarti, Editor (1998). *Reforming School Education*. New Delhi: Discovery Publishing House.

Bhaskara Rao, Digumarti, Editor (1998). *Teacher Education in India*. New Delhi: Discovery Publishing House.

Bhaskara Rao, Digumarti, Editor (1998). *World Summit for Social Development*. New Delhi: Discovery Publishing House.

Bhaskara Rao, Digumarti, Editor (2000). *Education for All: Achieving the Goal*, 3 Volumes. New Delhi: APH Publishing Corporation.

Vol. I *The Global Consensus*.

Vol. II *Mid-Decade Review Reports of Regional Seminars*.

Vol. III *Issues and Trends*.

Bhaskara Rao, Digumarti, Editor (2000), *International Encyclopedia of AIDS*, 11 Volumes in 13 parts. New Delhi: Discovery Publishing House.

Vol. 1 *Introduction to HIV/AIDS.*

Vol. 2 *HIV/AIDS—Issues and Challenges, 2 Parts.*

Vol. 3 *HIV/AIDS—Socio Economic Realities.*

Vol. 5 *AIDS and NGOs.*

Vol. 4 HIV / AIDS and Law, Ethics and Human Rights, 2 Parts.

Vol. 6 *AIDS and Home Care.*

Vol. 7 *STD Case Management.*

Vol. 8 *HIV/AIDS Prevention and Care—Teaching Modules for Nurses and Midwives.*

Vol. 9 *HIV Prevention Education for Education for Educational Institutions.*

Vol. 10 *Instructional Modules for AIDS Education.*

Vol. 11 *School Health Education to Prevent AIDS and STD—A Package for Curriculum Planners.*

Bhaskara Rao, Digumarti, Editor (2000). *International Encyclopedia of Science and Technology Education*, 11 Volumes. New Delhi: Discovery Publishing House.

Vol. 1 *Science and Technology Education.*

Vol. 2 *Science Education in Developing Countries.*

Vol. 3 *Organisational Structure of Science.*

Vol. 4 *Science Education in Asia and the Pacific.*

Vol. 5 *Science and Technology Education for All.*

Vol. 6 *Values, Ethics, Talent and Girls in Science and Technology Education.*

Vol. 7 *Popularization of Science and Technology Education.*

Vol. 8 *Science, Power and Society.*

Vol. 9 *Information Technology.*

Vol. 10 *Teacher Training in Science and Technology Education Framework.*

Vol. 11 *Science, Technology and Society: A Curriculum Framework.*

Bhaskara Rao, Digumarti, Editor (2001). *Distance Education in Different Countries*. New Delhi: APH Publishing Corporation.

Bhaskara Rao, Digumarti, Editor (2001). *Decentralised Management of Education: Management of Education in Panchayati Raj and Municipal Bodies*. New Delhi: Discovery Publishing House.

Bhaskara Rao, Digumarti, Editor (2001). *Electrochemistry for Environmental Protection*. New Delhi: Discovery Publishing House.

Bhaskara Rao, Digumarti, Editor (2001). *Global Educational Studies*. New Delhi: Discovery Publishing House.

Bhaskara Rao, Digumarti, Editor (2001). *Global Synthesis of Educational Assessment*. New Delhi: Discovery Publishing House.

Bhaskara Rao, Digumarti, Editor (2001). *International Encyclopedia of Human Rights*, 7 Volumes in 13 Parts. New Delhi: Discovery Publishing House.

Vol. 1 *International Instruments of Human Rights*, 2 Parts.

Vol. 2 *Regional Instruments of Human Rights*.

Vol. 3 *Human Rights and the United Nations*, 2 Parts.

Vol. 4 *Fact Files of Human Rights, 2 Parts*.

Vol. 5 *Study Stories of Human Rights, 3 Parts*.

Vol. 6 *International Meetings on Human Rights*, 2 Parts.

Vol. 7 *Professional Training in Human Rights*.

Bhaskara Rao, Digumarti, Editor (2001). *Jomtein Decade of Education*. New Delhi: Discovery Publishing House.

Bhaskara Rao, Digumarti, Editor (2001). *Nuclear Materials: Issues and Concerns*, 2 Volumes. New Delhi: Discovery Publishing House.

Bhaskara Rao, Digumarti, Editor (2001). *World Conference on Education for All*. New Delhi: APH Publishing Corporation.

Bhaskara Rao, Digumarti, Editor (2001). *World Conference on Higher Education*. New Delhi: Discovery Publishing House.

Bhaskara Rao, Digumarti, Editor (2001). *World Conference on Science*. New Delhi: Discovery Publishing House.

Bhaskara Rao, Digumarti, Editor (2003). *Inspiring Experiences in Teacher Education*. New Delhi: Discovery Publishing House.

Bhaskara Rao, Digumarti, Editor (2003). *International Studies in Education*, 3 Volumes. New Delhi: Discovery Publishing House.

Bhaskara Rao, Digumarti, Editor (2003). *Military Conversion: Impact on Science and Technology*. New Delhi: Discovery Publishing House.

Bhaskara Rao, Digumarti, Editor (2003). *United Nations Millennium Summit*. New Delhi: Discovery Publishing House.

Bhaskara Rao, Digumarti, Editor (2003). *World Assembly on Aging*. New Delhi: Discovery Publishing House.

Bhaskara Rao, Digumarti, Editor (2003). *World Conference on Human Rights*. New Delhi: Discovery Publishing House.

Bhaskara Rao, Digumarti, Editor (2003). *World Education Forum*. New Delhi: Discovery Publishing House.

Bhaskara Rao, Digumarti, Editor (2003). *Education Employment and Human Resource Development*. New Delhi: Discovery Publishing House.

Bhaskara Rao, Digumarti, Editor (2004). *Learning to Live Together*, 3 Volumes. New Delhi: Discovery Publishing House.

Bhaskara Rao, Digumarti, Editor (2003). *Successful Schooling*. New Delhi: Discovery Publishing House.

Bhaskara Rao, Digumarti, Editor (2003). *European Education and Teachers*. New Delhi: Discovery Publishing House.

Bhaskara Rao, Digumarti, Editor (2003). *Teachers in a Changing World*. New Delhi: Discovery Publishing House.

Bhaskara Rao, Digumarti and Chandra Mohan (2003). *Student Participation in Sports and Games*. New Delhi: APH Publishing Corporation.

Bhaskara Rao, Digumarti, C.A.P. Swamy and B.S.V. Dutt (1997). *Self Evaluation in Student Teaching*. New Delhi: Discovery Publishing House.

Bhaskara Rao, Digumarti and Digumarti Pushpa Latha (1994). *Achievement in Biology*. New Delhi: Discovery Publishing House.

Bhaskara Rao, Digumarti, C. Sridevi and K. Vijaya (1995). *Achievement in Social Studies*. New Delhi: Discovery Publishing House.

Bhaskara Rao, Digumarti and Digumarti Pushpa Latha (1995). *Achievement in English*. New Delhi: Discovery Publishing House.

Bhaskara Rao, Digumarti and Digumarti Pushpa Latha (1994). *Achievement in Science*. New Delhi: Discovery Publishing House.

Bhaskara Rao, Digumarti and Digumarti Pushpa Latha (1995). *Achievement in Mathematics*. New Delhi: Discovery Publishing House.

Bhaskara Rao, Digumarti and Digumarti Pushpa Latha, Editors (1998). *International Encyclopaedia of Women*, 5 Volumes. New Delhi: Discovery Publishing House.

Vol. 1 *Status of World's Women.*

Vol. 2 *Women, Education and Empowerment.*

Vol. 3 *Women Challenges and Advancement.*

Vol. 4 *Women and Family Health.*

Vol. 5 *Women and International Action.*

Bhaskara Rao, Digumarti, Digumarti Pushpa Latha and Digumarti Harshitha, Editors (2001). *Biological Warfare*. New Delhi: Discovery Publishing House.

Bhaskara Rao, Digumarti, Digumarti Pushpa Latha and Digumarti Harshitha, Editors (2001). *Women as Educators*. New Delhi: Discovery Publishing House.

Bhaskara Rao, Digumarti and Digumarti Harshitha, Editors (2001). *Education in India*. New Delhi: APH Publishing Corporation.

Bhaskara Rao, Digumarti, Digumarti Pushpa Latha and Digumarti Harshitha, Editors (2001). *Assessing Learning Achievement*. New Delhi: Discovery Publishing House.

Bhaskara Rao, Digumarti, Digumarti Pushpa Latha and Digumarti Harshitha, Editors (2001). *Energy Security*. New Delhi: Discovery Publishing House.

Bhaskara Rao, Digumarti, D. Harshitha and K.R.S.S. Rao, Editors (1999). *Advanced Biotechnology*. New Delhi: Discovery Publishing House.

Bhaskara Rao, Digumarti and D. Sridhar (2002). *Job Satisfaction of School Teachers*. New Delhi: Discovery Publishing House.

Bhaskara Rao, Digumarti and K.R.S. Sambasiva Rao, Editors (1996). *Current Trends in Indian Education*. New Delhi: Discovery Publishing House.

Bhaskara Rao, Digumarti and K. Vijaya (1995). *A Text Book of Evaluation*. Ambala Cantt: The Associated Publishers.

Bhaskara Rao, Digumarti and N.V.M. Mohana Rao (2003). *Problems of Mentally Handicapped Children*. New Delhi: Discovery Publishing House.

Bhaskara Rao, Digumarti, V.V. Rao, V.V. Lakshmi and V.V. Krishna, Editors (1999). *Status and Advancement of Women*. New Delhi: APH Publishing Corporation.

Babu, P.C. and Digumarti Bhaskara Rao, Editor (2003). *Flowers of Wisdom*. New Delhi: Discovery Publishing House.

Bhagya Lakshmi, Lingineni and Digumarti Bhaskara Rao, Editor (2000). *Reading and Comprehension*. New Delhi: Discovery Publishing House.

Bhuvaneswara Lakshmi, Gadde and Digumarti Bhaskara Rao, Editors (2000). *Attitude Towards Science*. New Delhi: Discovery Publishing House.

Devraj, T.A.S. and Digumarti Bhaskara Rao, Editor (1997). *Trace Analysis of Uranium and Thorium*. New Delhi: Discovery Publishing House.

Durga Rani, K. and Digumarthi Bhaskara Rao, Editor (2000). *Educational Aspirations and Scientific Attitudes*. New Delhi: Discovery Publishing House.

Dutt, B.S.V. and Digumarti Bhaskara Rao (2001). *Empowering Primary Teachers*. New Delhi: Discovery Publishing House.

Ediger, Marlow and Digumarti Bhaskara Rao (1996). *Science Curriculum*. New Delhi: Discovery Publishing House.

Ediger, Marlow and Digumarti Bhaskara Rao (2000). *Teaching Mathematics Successfully*. New Delhi: Discovery Publishing House.

Ediger, Marlow and Digumarti Bhaskara Rao (2001). *Teaching Science Successfully*. New Delhi: Discovery Publishing House.

Ediger, Marlow and Digumarti Bhaskara Rao (2001). *Teaching Social Studies Successfully*. New Delhi: Discovery Publishing House.

Ediger, Marlow and Digumarti Bhaskara Rao (2003). *Philosophy and Curriculum*. New Delhi: Discovery Publishing House.

Ediger, Marlow and Digumarti Bhaskara Rao (2003). *Psychology and Curriculum*. New Delhi: Discovery Publishing House.

Ediger, Marlow and Digumarti Bhaskara Rao (2003). *Improving School Administration*. New Delhi: Discovery Publishing House.

Ediger, Marlow and Digumarti Bhaskara Rao (2003). *School Curriculum and Administration*. New Delhi: Discovery Publishing House.

Ediger, Marlow and Digumarti Bhaskara Rao (2003). *Elementary Curriculum*. New Delhi: Discovery Publishing House.

Ediger, Marlow and Digumarti Bhaskara Rao (2003). *Language Arts Curriculum*. New Delhi: Discovery Publishing House.

Ediger, Marlow and Digumarti Bhaskara Rao (2003). *Teaching Language Arts Successfully*. New Delhi: Discovery Publishing House.

Ediger, Marlow and Digumarti Bhaskara Rao (2003). *Teaching Mathematics in Elementary Schools*. New Delhi: Discovery Publishing House.

Ediger, Marlow and Digumarti Bhaskara Rao (2003). *Teaching Science in Elementary Schools*. New Delhi: Discovery Publishing House.

Ediger, Marlow and Digumarti Bhaskara Rao (2004). *Teaching Social Studies in Elementary Schools*. New Delhi: Discovery Publishing House.

Ediger, Marlow, B.S.V. Dutt and Digumarti Bhaskara Rao (2003). *Teaching English Successfully*. New Delhi: Discovery Publishing House.

Jayasree, Kandi and Digumarti Bhaskara Rao, Editor (1999). *Correlates of Socialisation*. New Delhi: Discovery Publishing House.

John Babu, Ch. and T.J.R. Prasad, G.M. Madhukar and Digumarti Bhaskara Rao, Editors (1996). *Problems Solving in Mathematics*. New Delhi: APH Publishing Corporation.

Jyothi, Nirmala and Digumarti Bhaskara Rao, Editor (2003). *Non-Detention System in School Education*. New Delhi: Discovery Publishing House.

Marja, Talvi and Digumarti Bhaskara Rao, Editors (1996). *Educational Leadership and Social Changes*. New Delhi: Discovery Publishing House.

Prabhakaram, K.S. and Digumarti Bhaskara Rao, Editors (1998). *Concept Attainment Model in Mathematics Teaching*. New Delhi: Discovery Publishing House.

Prasanth Kumar, J. and Digumarti Bhaskara Rao, Editor (1998). *Effectiveness of Distance Education System*. New Delhi: Discovery Publishing House.

Prasanth Kumar, J. and Digumarti Bhaskara Rao, and G. Sundara Rao, Editors (2000). *Open University Student Support Services*. New Delhi: Discovery Publishing House.

Ramatulasamma, K. and Digumarti Bhaskara Rao, Editor (2003). *Job Satisfaction of Teacher Educators*. New Delhi: Discovery Publishing House.

Ramakrishnaiah, D. and Digumarti Bhaskara Rao, Editor (1998). *Job Satisfaction of College Teachers*. New Delhi: Discovery Publishing House.

Rathaiah, Lavu and Digumarti Bhaskara Rao, Editors (1996). *International Innovations in Education*. New Delhi: Discovery Publishing House.

Rathaiah, Lavu and Digumarti Bhaskara Rao (1997). *Achievement Correlates*. New Delhi: Discovery Publishing House.

Ramesh, Ganta and Digumarti Bhaskara Rao, Editors (1998). *Environmental Education: Problems and Prospects*. New Delhi: Discovery Publishing House.

Reddy, Sudhakar and Digumarti Bhaskara Rao, Editor (2003). *Creativity in Adolescents*. New Delhi: Discovery Publishing House.

Reddy, M.S. and Digumarti Bhaskara Rao, Editor (2003). *Creativity in College Students*. New Delhi: Discovery Publishing House.

Rudramamba, B. and Digumarti Bhaskara Rao, Editor (2004). *Problems of Teaching*. New Delhi: APH Publishing Corporation.

Sanjeeva Rao, P.C. and Digumarti Bhaskara Rao, Editor (1996). *A Text Book of Geology*. New Delhi: Discovery Publishing House.

Satya Narayana, V and Digumarti Bhaskara Rao, Editor (2001). *Physical Education, Social Attitudes and Leadership Qualities*. New Delhi: Discovery Publishing House.

Srinivasulu Reddy, M. K.R.S. Sambasiva Rao and Digumarti Bhaskara Rao, Editor (1999). *A Text Book of Aquaculture*. New Delhi: Discovery Publishing House.

Srinivasa Rao, M. and Digumarti Bhaskara Rao, Editor (2003). *Achievement Motivation and Achievement in Mathematics*. New Delhi: Discovery Publishing House.

Vanaja, M. and Digumarti Bhaskara Rao, Editor (1999). *Inquiry Training Model*. New Delhi: Discovery Publishing House.

Valeri V. Koustiouk and Digumarti Bhaskara Rao, Editor (2003). *A Text Book of Cryogenics*. New Delhi: Discovery Publishing House.

Veena Kumari, Balusu and Digumarti Bhaskara Rao, (1996). *Operation Black Board*. New Delhi: Ashish Publishing House.

Veena Kumari, Balusu and Digumarti Bhaskara Rao, Editor (2000). *Psycho-Social Correlates of Achievement*. New Delhi: Discovery Publishing House.

Venkata Rao, P. and Digumarti Bhaskara Rao (1989). *A Text Book of Zoology—Junior Intermediate*. Guntur: Vignan Publishers.

Venkata Rao, P. and Digumarti Bhaskara Rao (1989). *A Text Book of Zoology—Senior Intermediate*. Guntur: Vignan Publishers.

Venugopala Rao, K and Digumarti Bhaskara Rao, Editor (2002). *Teacher Morale in Secondary Schools*. New Delhi: Discovery Publishing House.

Vidya, C. and Digumarti Bhaskara Rao, Editor (1996). *A Text Book of Nutrition*. New Delhi: Discovery Publishing House.

Vidya Bharathi, D. and Digumarti Bhaskara Rao, Editor (2000). *Educational Philosophies of Swami Vivekanand and John Dewey*. New Delhi: APH Publishing Corporation.

Vidya, C. and Digumarti Bhaskara Rao, Editor (1996). *A Text Book of Nutrition*. New Delhi: Discovery Publishing House.

Bhaskara Rao Digumarti (1986). *Dhrushya Sravana Bodhanapakaranalu* (Audio Visual Teaching Aids). Guntur: Nagarjuna Publishers.

Bhaskara Rao, Digumarti (1993). *Jeevasashtra Bodhana* (Teaching of Biology). Guntur: Nagarjuna Publishers.

Bhaskara Rao, Digumarti (1995). *Vignanasasthra Bodhana* (Teaching of Science). Guntur: Nagarjuna Publishers.

Bhaskara Rao, Digumarti (1997). *Vidya Manovignana Seshtram* (Educational Psychology). Guntur: Creative Press.

Bhaskara Rao, Digumarti (1998). *DSC Study Material*. Guntur: Nagarjuna Publishers.

Bhaskara Rao, Digumarti (1998). *Upadhyayudu Vidya* (Teacher and Education). Guntur: Nagarjuna Publishers.

Bhaskara Rao, Digumarti (1998). *Vidya Drukpadalu* (Perspectives of Education). Guntur: Nagarjuna Publishers.

Bhaskara Rao, Digumarti (1999). *EdCET Teaching Aptitude*. Guntur: Nagarjuna Publishers.

Bhaskara Rao, Digumarti (2001). *Bharata Samajamulo Upadyayudu Vidya* (Teacher and Education in Emerging Indian Society). Guntur: Nagarjuna Publishers.

Bhaskara Rao, Digumarti (2001). *Bhoutika Sastra Bodhana Paddathulu* (Methods of Teaching Physical Science). Guntur: Nagarjuna Publishers.

Bhaskara Rao, Digumarti (2001). *Jeeva Sastra Bodhana Paddathulu* (Methods of Teaching Biology). Guntur: Nagarjuna Publishers.

Bhaskara Rao, Digumarti (2001). *Vidya Manovignana Sastram* (Educational Psychology). Guntur: Nagarjuna Publishers.

Bhaskara Rao, Digumarti. (2003). *Patasala Yajamanyam Paripalana* (School Management and Administration). Guntur: Nagarjuna Publishers.

Bhaskara Rao, Digumarti (2003). *Vidya Sanketika Sastram Mariyu Computer Vidya* (Educational Technology and Computer Education). Guntur: Nagarjuna Publishers.

Index

Administrator as instructional Leader, 77-82
- Instructional leadership, 77-79
- Problems in teaching-learning situations, 80-82
- Role of, 79, 80, 83

Aristotle, 19

Bacon, Francis, 19

Behaviourism, 51, 53

Bruner, Jerome, 79

Counsellor in school curriculum, 120-25
- Counsellors assistance and guidance, 124-25
- Problems experienced by students, 120-24
  - Drug abuse, 123-24
  - Feeling of security, 122
  - Loneliness, 121
  - Physiological needs unmet, 123

Criterion reference test, 54

Darwin, Charles, 68, 69

Dennis, 112

Dewey, John, 67

Existentialism, 26, 27

Experimentalism, 25

Froebal, Friedrich Wilhelm, 101-03, 108

Grant, WT, 7

Herbart, Johann Friedrich, 67

Huxley, Thomas Hensy, 68, 75

Idealism, 25, 26

In service education, 15, 21
- Decision making stills for students, 18, 20, 21
- Idea centred curriculum, 17, 18, 21
- Looking to past for direction, 18, 19
- Problem solving in curriculum, 16, 17, 21
- Testing and measurement movement, 15, 16, 21

Integrated science curriculum, 66-75
- Contract system, 74
- Correlation in teaching, 67
- Decision-making, 73, 74
- Learning centres, 74
- Modern science curriculum, 69, 74
- Objectives in, 72, 73
- Object lessons in teaching, 66
- Problem solving, 67, 72
- Scope, 66
- Separate subjects curriculum, 66
- Teaching strategy, 75

Jarolimek, John, 140

Kansky, 112

Kindergarten education, 101-08

History of, 101-03

Measurement driven instruction, 106-07

Open curriculum in, 103-05

Philosophies of, 107-08

Subject centred curriculum, 105-06

Lancaster, Joseph, 66, 74

Lancasterian monitorial system of instruction, 66

Maslow, AH, 142

Microcomputer use in classroom, 109-19

Improving software quality, 113-16

Student microcomputer ratio, 109-10

Teacher and, 110-13

Teacher developed software, 116-17

Utilization, 117-18

Parent teacher conferences and the pupil, 91-94

Expanding use of, 92-94

Setting for the conference, 91-92

Pestalozzi, Johann Friederich, 66

Philosophy of education, 25

Philosophy of teaching the rural student, 31-33

Plaget, Jean, 79

Plato, 19

Problem solving and school administration, 26, 34

Administrator face, 126-27

Curriculum and, 128-29

Discipline and, 127-28

In service education, 130-31

Personal needs of teachers and, 131-33

School attendance and the principal, 129-30

Realism, 26

Remedying ills in society, 84, 90

Additional problems in society, 85-90

Child abuse, 86-87

Economic competency, 84, 85

Public school curriculum, 89, 90

Public schools to, 84, 87, 90

Sexually transmitted disease, 87

Students from poverty homes, 86

Rogers Carl, 142

Roussean, Jean Jacque, 68, 75

Rural school curriculum, 29-34

Philosophy of teaching, 31-33

Rural students need, 33

Students and, 29-31, 33, 34

School administration and curriculum, 35-43

Caution on recommendations, 40-42

Role of administration in school setting, 35, 40, 42

Basic skills, 38

Competency based instruction, 39

Mastery learning, 38, 39

Time on task, 38

School library, 135-43

Criteria for use, 137-39

Individual differences, 135-36

Instructional materials centres, 136-37

Philosophy of services, 141-42

Quality library, 142-43

Use and location of reference materials, 139-41

School secretary, 95-100

Competent, 98-99

Quality environment, 95-97

Responsibility and, 97, 98

Snygg, Donald, 142

Social studies, 51-57

Issues needing resolving in, 57

Problems in, 57

Recommendations in teaching of, 51-57

Spencer Herbert, 69, 75

SR theory of learning, 67, 68

Student motivation in reading, 44-50

Recommendations to improve reading curriculum, 48, 50

Why motivation, 44, 45

Why motivation lacking, 45, 48

Students reentry into curriculum, 7, 14

Curriculum for, 10, 14

Identification of perspectives, 8, 10

Students entering workplace with formal schooling, 7

Thorndike, EL, 67

Upgraded school administrators, 1, 6

Needed administrators with positive attitude, 4, 5

Needed knowledge administrators, 1, 2

Needed moral standards and professional behaviour in schools, 5

Needed school administrators with social skills, 3, 4

Recommendations to improve schools, 5, 6

Urban school curriculum, 23, 28

Philosophy of education, 25, 27

Principles of learning and, 23, 25

Urban students need for experience, 27, 28